Football's Attacking Combination-60 Defense

FOOTBALL'S ATTACKING COMBINATION-60 DEFENSE

Bob Kenig

PARKER PUBLISHING COMPANY, INC.

WEST NYACK, NEW YORK

Library of Congress Cataloging in Publication Data

Kenig, Bob.
  Football's attacking combination-60 defense.

  Includes index.
  1. Football–Defense.   2. Football–Offense.
3. Football coaching.   I. Title   II. Title:
Football's attacking combination-sixty defense.
GV951.18.K46   796.332′2   81-14100
ISBN 0-13-323780-2   AACR2

Printed in the United States of America

To the three S's in my life: Sandy, my wife, and Stacy and Shannon, our two daughters. Without their love and understanding, this book and my career would have never been possible.

and

To my parents, Pat and Anna, who taught me the value of hard work and gave me the desire to succeed.

Foreword

If you truly believe the adage that "defense wins in football," then Bob Kenig's book will be right down your alley. If you don't believe the premise, then by all means read this text, so you won't be shocked by your opponents who read and utilize the material enclosed in Coach Kenig's very intriguing reference, *Football's Attacking Combination-60 Defense.*

This defense is designed for not only the average high school team but for teams on all levels. The coach utilizing it should not only be able to keep pressure on the offenses he faces, but most certainly will be able to shut down his opponents' scoring abilities. For example, Coach Kenig employed the Combination-60 Defense in leading Marple Newtown to the top of Pennsylvania's high school football circles. He tells it all for your edification in this book. By making use of a limited number of skills (simplicity for individuals), and then combining them (complexity for opponents), the coach employing the "60" has a tough defensive arsenal at his disposal.

I have had the good fortune to see personally Bob Kenig's attention and thoroughness to detail during the past two years that he has been a member of our staff. Coach Kenig had complete charge of our scouting operation, and his chapter on scouting is worth the price of the book alone. In fact, the scouting material, if incorporated into your program, might well improve your game planning a hundred-fold.

A successful, very dedicated coach, Bob Kenig has assembled a most technical guide for the Combination-60

Defense. The value of his material is enhanced by details of the practice schedule he used and the suggested drilling methods for teaching this system. If you believe in Kenig's approach of taking an average player, training him thoroughly, and motivating him, then you will find this book most beneficial. In fact, even the coach of the most sophisticated defense will find the comprehensive material in the book extremely valuable.

Enthusiastic, hard-working Bob Kenig has endeavored throughout his entire coaching career to increase his knowledge of football. Now, through this book, he passes along to you the labors of his entire professional career. I am pleased to highly recommend it for your reading and utilization.

Bill Manlove
Head Football Coach and Athletic Director
Widener University

ADVANTAGES OF
THE COMBINATION-60

The Combination-60 Defense is geared to the abilities of the average athlete; it does not depend on the talents of the exceptional athlete to achieve success. Speed and aggressiveness are more important ingredients than size and strength.

In the Combination-60, the smaller, quicker athletes are effective for several reasons. A defensive lineman is never called upon to align on an offensive lineman and read and react to his movements. He is coached to attack a particular area along the line of scrimmage on the snap of the ball, and to fight to control that area before reacting to the play. This attacking technique is effectively executed by an aggressive, quick athlete.

The attacking technique employed by the defensive linemen occupies and often confuses the offensive blockers. This protects the linebackers and keeps the blockers off them. This eliminates the need for the big, strong linebackers that are such a vital part of many modern defenses.

When an athlete combines size and strength with speed and aggressiveness, he is a more effective performer in the Combination-60 than a smaller, weaker athlete. This is true in any defensive scheme. However, in most defenses size and strength are requirements; in the Combination-60, it is beneficial to possess these qualities but they are not required for individual or team success.

The Combination-60 Defense is geared, not only to the physical abilities, but to the mental abilities of the average

player. For the individual player, his techniques and responsibilities are uncomplicated and easily understood.
This is accomplished by giving our defensive linemen only
two basic alignments and two charge techniques. Our
linebackers learn one basic alignment and our secondary
plays very uncomplicated three-deep zone and man-to-
man coverages.

As simple as the defense is to learn and teach, it
appears to be very complex and causes much confusion for
our opponents. This confusion is primarily accomplished
by the alignments and charge techniques of our defensive
line. The placement of our linebackers and the various
secondary coverages adds to the confusion. The Combina-
tion-60 Defense has eliminated confusion for our team and
created it for our opponents.

The Combination-60 is equally effective against both
the run and the pass. The defense was developed to handle
the increased rushing attacks of our opponents, especially
the various elements of the option play. Even though the
defense employs an eight-man front, it possesses the
elements that are necessary to cope with all passing
attacks. It is particularly effective against wide passing
actions such as sprint-out, rollout, and play action. This is
partially due to the double outside pass rush that is
employed against these wide passing attacks.

The Combination-60 Defense is designed for any high
school coach who does not have the athletes, year after
year, with the size and strength to overpower their opponents. The defense is for the coach who wants to make
defense as imaginative and as exciting as any modern
offense. It is for all coaches who get the average, rather
than the exceptional, football players; and who want to
make defensive football more fun, more aggressive, and
more successful for their players as well as themselves.

This book contains all aspects of the Combination-60
Defense. It includes the interior line placements as well as
a complete explanation of the "Slant" and "Up" charges,
which are the backbone of the defense. The linebacker,
defensive end, and secondary play are completely covered.

The scouting system is outlined and its relationship to the defensive game plan is explained. Also included are the drills that were developed for the Combination-60. Organization of the defensive practice is thoroughly covered. Most importantly, defensive adjustments during the game are covered in depth.

Since this book does contain all aspects of the Combination-60, it should be read completely to acquire an understanding of all concepts. The book should then be referred to periodically to reinforce the understanding of these concepts.

BOB KENIG

ACKNOWLEDGMENTS

I owe a great deal of thanks to:

All my assistant coaches, especially Fred McKonly, Jim Schmidt, and Tom Wimer. They are what every assistant coach should be.

Bill Manlove, the finest coach I have ever known.

Harry Miller, who gave me my first coaching position.

Lou Bonder, my high school coach, who instilled in me the desire to be a coach.

Karen Moore and Roberta Hobson, who spent countless hours typing my manuscript.

All the young men who played for us and made the Combination-60 a great success.

TABLE OF CONTENTS

ADVANTAGES OF THE COMBINATION-60   9

**1. REASONS FOR THE COMBINATION-60
DEFENSE** 19

Defensive Personnel • (19)
   Defensive Line
   Linebackers
Changes in Opponents' Attacks • (21)
   Increased Running
   Wide Passing Actions
Desire for a Unique Defense • (27)
   Characteristics of the Combination-60

**2. SELECTING DEFENSIVE PERSONNEL FOR
THE COMBINATION-60** 31

Testing Program • (32)
   Vertical Jump
   40-Yard Dash
   Push-ups
   Side-Stepping
   Mile and One-Half Run
Position Descriptions • (38)
   Guards
   Tackles
   Ends
   Linebackers
   Halfbacks
   Safety

**3. ALIGNMENT AND PLAY OF THE
COMBINATION-60 INTERIOR LINE** 43

Guards • (44)
   Stance

Alignment
Technique
Keys and Reactions
Run Responsibilities
Pass Responsibilities

Tackles • (55)
Stance
Alignment
Technique
Keys and Reactions
Run Responsibilities
Pass Responsibilities

**4. COACHING THE COMBINATION-60
LINEBACKERS AND DEFENSIVE ENDS 63**

Linebackers • (63)
Stance
Alignment
Keys and Reactions
Blitz Techniques
Run Responsibilities
Pass Responsibilities

Defensive Ends • (81)
Stance
Alignment
Keys and Reactions
Run Responsibilities
Pass Responsibilities

**5. ALIGNMENT AND PLAY OF THE
COMBINATION-60 SECONDARY 89**

Halfback • (89)
Stance
Alignment
Keys and Reactions
Run Responsibilities
Pass Responsibilities

Safety • (101)
Stance
Alignment

    Keys and Reactions
    Run Responsibilities
    Pass Responsibilities

6. COMBINATION-60 TEAM DEFENSES 113

Defensive Calls • (119)

Front Defenses • (121)
    Slant
    Up

Secondary • (125)
    Corner
    Invert
    Stay
    Free Safety
    Man-to-Man

7. COMBINATION DEFENSES 141

Defensive Calls • (144)

Various Combinations • (145)

Game Specials • (146)

Goal-Line and Short-Yardage Defenses • (147)
    Gap
    Tough

8. THE COMBINATION-60 DEFENSE
IN ACTION 155

Off-Tackle Play • (155)
    Team Defenses
    Combination Defense

Option Play • (160)
    Team Defenses
    Combination Defense

Trap Play • (167)
    Team Defenses
    Combination Defense

Sprint Pass • (170)
    Team Defenses
    Combination Defense

9. THE COMBINATION-60 SCOUTING SYSTEM AND DEFENSIVE GAME PLAN..................175

Organization of the Scouting System • (175)

Various Scouting Charts • (180)
  Formation and Play
  Down and Distance, Field Position
  Individual Pass and Run Summary
  Offensive Personnel

Coordinating the Scouting Report and the Defensive Game Plan • (192)

Adjusting the Defensive Game Plan During the Game • (194)

Post-Game Evaluation • (196)

10. THE COMBINATION-60 DRILLS AND DEFENSIVE PRACTICE SCHEDULE 199

Stretch Period • (200)

Individual Period • (200)
  Defensive Line
  Linebackers and Ends
  Secondary

First Kicking Period • (213)

Teaching Period • (213)

Group Period • (214)
  Defensive Line
  Linebackers and Ends
  Secondary

Halftime • (218)

Combo • (218)
  Defensive Line

Team • (220)

Second Kicking Period • (221)

Rope Jumping and Weight Lifting • (222)

INDEX **223**

REASONS FOR THE
COMBINATION-60 DEFENSE

1

There were two main reasons for the development of the Combination-60 Defense. The defense was a solution to many problems that developed while employing a basic Pro 4-3 defense. (Diagram 1-1). These problems were caused by an overall decrease in the size of our defensive personnel and by changes that were occurring in the offensive attacks of our opponents. This was the most important reason for the development of the defense.

The second reason for the defense was to fulfill our desire to build a defensive package of unique qualities, and to present our opponents with a defensive attack that they had never before seen.

DEFENSIVE PERSONNEL

Defensive Line

The decrease in the size of our defensive personnel began to cause us some serious defensive problems. We had employed the Pro 4-3 for sometime and had enjoyed

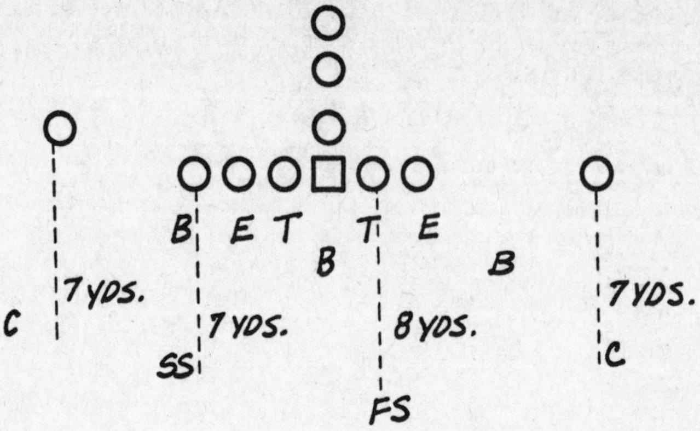

DIAGRAM 1-1

much success with it. During that period, our defensive line averaged over 200 pounds and was rarely over-matched in size by the offensive lines of our opponents. This size advantage helped our linemen in their responsibility of reading the movements of the offensive line, and then reacting to those movements. Our size and strength prohibited most offensive blockers from moving any defensive lineman off the line of scrimmage prior to or during the process of reading and reacting to the movement of that blocker.

Our smaller defensive linemen were not enjoying the same success. They were often much smaller than the offensive blockers they faced. Even though the smaller defenders were quicker than our larger defensive linemen of the past, they were being overpowered at the line of scrimmage while attempting to read and react to the movements of the offensive line. This was especially true when our opponents used straight-ahead drive blocks. This problem was causing our defensive linemen to lose some of their aggressiveness. We also felt this problem was causing the linemen to lose confidence in both the defensive system and the ability of the coaches to develop a system that could effectively stop our opponents.

Linebackers

The problems caused by the decrease in size were not unique to the defensive line. The linebackers suffered from the same problem. When our outside linebackers played on a tight end, they were often overmatched in size and were being blocked off the ball by him. The middle linebacker was often faced with the same problem when the center blocked straight ahead on him. Even though the smaller, quicker linebackers were more effective on pass coverage, they were less effective against the run.

To compensate for lack of size, we employed a linebacker blitz. We believed that getting a defender quickly in the offensive backfield could easily disrupt an offensive play and give our defenders a better opportunity to stop the play. As much as we liked getting a defender quickly into the offensive backfield, we were hesitant to employ this weapon often. When the blitzing linebacker did not succeed in disrupting the offensive play, the defense was weakened against the run and pass.

CHANGES IN OPPONENTS' ATTACKS

Increased Running

With the emphasis being placed on a successful running attack by numerous colleges and universities, our opponents began increasing the running phases of their attacks. Our seven-man defensive front, along with the decrease in size of our defensive personnel, was not stopping the running attacks consistently.

We experimented by using a monster concept in the secondary (Diagram 1-2). This put eight men close to the line of scrimmage as opposed to the seven men we had been using. While this aided the defense of the run, it weakened our defense to the side away from the monster. We liked the idea of an eight-man front, but we did not like being stronger to one side than the other.

Wide Passing Actions

With the increased emphasis on the running game, our opponents were getting away from the use of dropback passing and were using wide passing actions such as the sprint-out, rollout, and play action. We felt the Pro 4-3, with a four-deep secondary, was not providing us with a

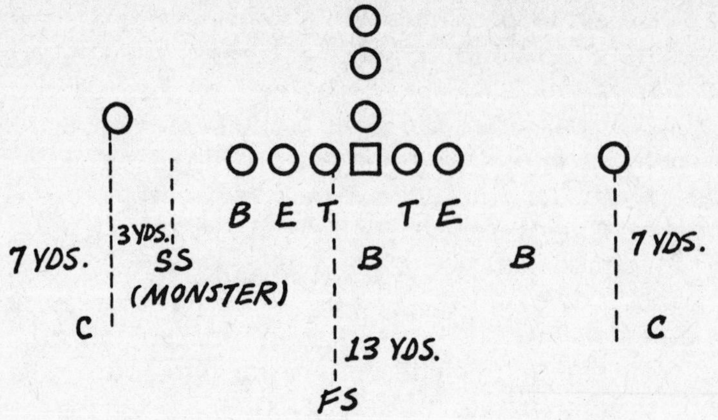

DIAGRAM 1-2

sufficient outside pass rush to deal with this type of attack. The defensive tackle and end to the side of the passing action were being attacked by the offensive guard and the tackle. The outside linebacker was being attacked by a back. This meant that we had three rushers and our opponents had three blockers to handle them. When the offensive back effectively blocked our outside linebacker, the quarterback was left with two options. He could take time to find his receiver and throw the ball, or he could run and force the corner. This put the defensive back responsible for the flat zone in a bind. When he attacked the quarterback, he left the flat zone uncovered and the quarterback could hit a receiver in that zone. When he held his ground, he gave the quarterback room to run the ball (Diagram 1-3).

We were not only dissatisfied with our outside pass rush, we were displeased with our four-deep secondary coverage against the wide passing actions. We had a secondary man in the flat zone to the side of the passing action and a secondary defender in each of the deep one-third zones. We believed a defender in each of the three deep zones was normally necessary on dropback action but rarely necessary on a wide passing action. When our opponents employed a wide passing action, it was very rare for the quarterback to throw the ball into the deep

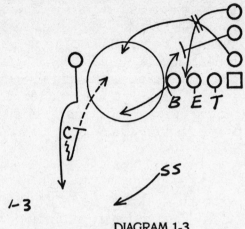

DIAGRAM 1-3

outside one-third zone opposite the direction of his wide passing action. Therefore, the defender in that deep outside zone was not being used efficiently (Diagram 1-4).

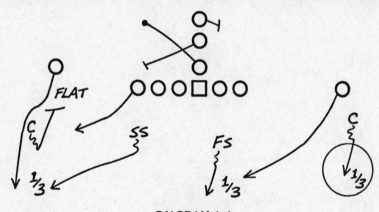

DIAGRAM 1-4

We also experimented with a variation of the monster secondary to give us both a better outside pass rush and a more efficient use of our secondary personnel. The side of the offensive formation to which the monster was placed was determined by our scouting report on the opponent. We placed him to the side where the opponent most often ran the football and the side to which the quarterback most often used a wide passing action.

When the quarterback employed a wide passing action to the side of the monster, the outside linebacker attacked the quarterback, and so did the monster. This provided an excellent double outside pass rush. We then rotated or leveled our secondary. This put the cornerback in the flat to the side of the wide passing action. The safety flowed to the deep outside one-third zone. The cornerback away from the passing action was responsible for the other two-thirds of the deep area.

Two factors aided the safety with his coverage of the deep outside one-third zone. The double outside pass rush forced the quarterback to throw the ball faster than he wanted to throw it. This seriously prohibited the wide receiver, to the side of the passing action, from running any deep patterns. This wide receiver was "bumped" by the cornerback as the cornerback moved into the flat zone. This also aided in prohibiting deep patterns to the wide receiver (Diagram 1-5).

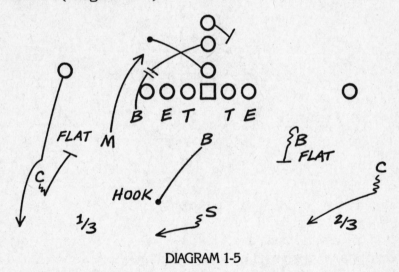

DIAGRAM 1-5

When the quarterback used a wide passing action away from the monster, we employed basically the same coverage. The cornerback, to the side of the passing action, covered the flat zone, while the safety covered the deep outside one-third zone to that side. The cornerback, away from the passing action, was again responsible for the other two-thirds of the deep area. The monster was responsible for the flat zone away from the passing action. This allowed the outside linebacker, to that side, to rush the quarterback (Diagram 1-6).

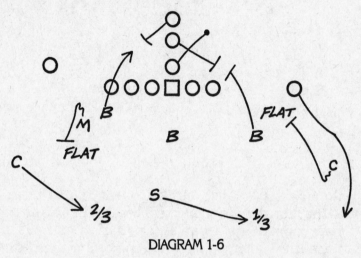

DIAGRAM 1-6

When the quarterback employed a dropback passing action, which was very rare, the monster covered the flat zone to his side. This again allowed the outside linebacker to rush the quarterback. The other flat zone was covered by the outside linebacker; the three deep zones were covered by the two cornerbacks and the safety (Diagram 1-7).

The monster idea was very effective when our opponent ran or used a wide passing action to the side of the monster. It was also effective against the dropback pass, but we were not satisfied with it when the opponent ran or used a wide passing action away from the monster.

When the opponent ran away from the monster, we were still a basic Pro 4-3 defense and even slightly weaker, since the free safety was playing more to the middle of the offensive formation. This alignment and depth made it more difficult for him to help effectively on a wide run to either side. Therefore, the monster concept gave us abso-

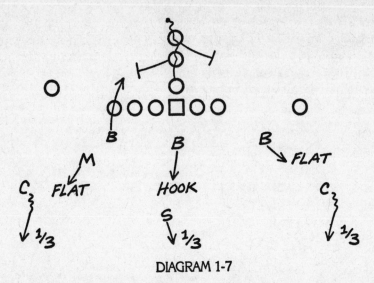

DIAGRAM 1-7

lutely no advantage when our opponent ran to the side opposite the monster. This problem became more apparent when many opponents began employing an "audible system" at the line of scrimmage and attacking the defense away from the monster (Diagram 1-8).

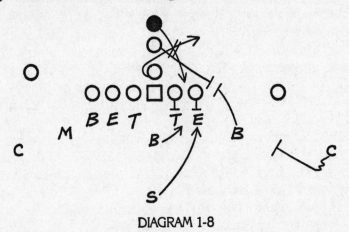

DIAGRAM 1-8

Even though we were satisfied with the monster pass coverage when the quarterback used a wide passing action away from the monster, we were not satisfied with the single outside pass rush. The monster eliminated the ineffective use of a pass defender in the deep outside one-third zone away from the wide passing action of the quarterback, but it provided only a double outside pass rush when the passing action was to the side of the monster.

DESIRE FOR A UNIQUE DEFENSE

We believed we could continue to work with the Pro 4-3 defensive concept and develop enough variations to overcome the problems we were encountering. Yet, even with numerous complicated variations and adjustments, we would still be using a defense that our opponents had seen and worked against for many years. We decided to work on the development of a new defense.

The first step was to decide on the characteristics we wanted our defense to possess. This first step was handled at a very long winter staff meeting, where we came up with the following requirements.

Characteristics of the Combination-60

1. Make use of the speed and the aggressiveness of our line and linebackers and not depend on size and strength.

2. Nearly eliminate the responsibility of reading and reacting to the movements of the offensive line by our defensive linemen.

3. Have a defender fire into the offensive backfield on every play without weakening the defense against the run or pass.

4. Cause confusion for our opponents by various alignments and attacks.

5. Be a balanced eight-man front, to cope with the increase in running by our opponents.

6. Protect our linebackers from blockers, so they are free to make tackles on all running plays.

7. Have the capability of attacking the wide passing action quarterback with two defenders from the outside.

8. Have a secondary that makes optimum use of the three deep defenders, while being flexible enough to handle all situations.

9. Be capable of handling all goal-line and short-yardage situations.

10. Make good use of all the information acquired from scouting.

11. Most importantly, be simple to teach for our coaches and be understood easily and executed by our players.

After numerous staff meetings, discussions with high school and college coaches, and experimentation with our players, the *Combination-60 Defense* was born.

The following are a few of the features of the Combination-60 Defense:

1. The interior linemen (guards and tackles) use two charge techniques. They are the *"Slant"* and the *"Up."* They can be executed to the left or to the right. When all the interior linemen execute the same technique, it is called a *Team Defense.* When some of the interior linemen execute a "Slant," while the others execute an "Up," it is a *Combination Defense.* Both charge techniques attack an offensive area and involve little reading.

2. The alignments and responsibilities of the linebackers and ends are determined by the direction of the *Defensive Call.* In nearly every defense, there is at least one linebacker or end who fires into the offensive backfield without weakening the entire defense in any way. This, along with the various line charges, causes confusion for the opponent.

3. The linebacker, end, guard, and tackle who are aligned on the side of the Defensive Call are called *onside.* For example, When "Slant-Right" is called, the right linebacker, end, guard, and tackle are onside. The other front defenders are *offside.*

4. The three deep secondarys employ four different zone coverages that are controlled by the action of the quarterback. The four coverages are Stay, Corner, Invert, and Free Safety. They also employ two different man-to-man coverages. One kind is used with both the Team and Combination defenses. The other is used with the short-yardage defenses that are known as *Gap* and *Tough*.

SELECTING DEFENSIVE PERSONNEL FOR THE COMBINATION-60

Discipline, desire, and pride are mental qualities that can be found, to a certain degree, in all human beings. Success is greatly determined by the extent to which these qualities are developed. The successful football player possesses these qualities and develops them to a high degree.

Quickness, strength, endurance, and explosiveness are physical qualities that are also found in all human beings. The degree to which the football player develops these qualities is also a factor in the achievement of success. These physical qualities can be measured, prior to the start of the season, by the use of a testing program. Even though there may be some type of test to measure the mental qualities, we rely primarily on the daily observation of the players to measure these.

Both the testing program and the daily observation of players help determine the team members that will be encouraged to play defense. We allow each player to select the position that he wishes to play. We encourage the majority of our best athletes to become members of the defensive unit, but we do not force them into it. We also allow the team members to change their positions at any time during the season. A football player wants to be in a position where he will be a starter or, at least, play a great deal. This freedom of position selection allows the players to evaluate all positions and select the one where he believes he has the best chance to play. This method of personnel placement has worked extremely well for us. Normally, our best athletes do select the defensive unit, and those athletes who are slightly behind them in athletic ability select the offense. This has allowed our best 22 players to be starters on the offensive and defensive units, without having any player feel that he was forced to play a position he did not want to play.

TESTING PROGRAM

The testing program, though not foolproof, gives a good indication of a player's athletic ability. It also gives a good indication of the amount of work a player has done in preparation for the season. This also provides an indication of the mental qualities of the players. Players who have worked extremely hard to get into good physical condition certainly have more discipline, desire, and pride than those who are in poor physical shape.

On the first day of fall practice, the testing program is administered. The team is divided into groups according to the positions they initially select. The four groups are the backs and receivers, linebackers, ends and defensive backs, offensive line, and defensive line. Testing the athletes in these groups serves two purposes. It gives all players some idea concerning the abilities of those people against whom they must compete for a starting job. It also encourages everyone to do their best in an effort to impress their peers. Players are also encouraged to do their best because the test is administered by the coach or coaches who handle that group during the season. The athletes certainly want to perform well for those men who will teach and evaluate them during the season.

The test consists of five parts; each part is a station within the testing circuit. The groups complete the first four stations, which are the 40-yard dash, push-ups, side-stepping, and vertical jump, then finish with the mile and one-half run. Each group starts at one of the first four parts and then finishes with the run. The order of events are as follows:

1. Vertical Jump
2. 40-Yard Dash
3. Push-Ups
4. Side-Stepping
5. Mile and One-Half Run

It is not necessary to start with number one as long as the correct order is followed throughout the first four parts. In other words, if a group starts at number four, they must follow with one, two, three, and then five. The team is instructed to wear gym shorts and sneakers. For the 40-yard dash, they are allowed to wear football or track shoes if they wish.

There are a minimum number of points that each player must score in order to pass the test. A player who cannot reach this score will not get a uniform until he passes the test. We believe the athlete who cannot reach this minimum standard could easily become injured as a result of poor conditioning. At Widener University the minimum score is 32.5 points. While coaching in high school, we used 27.5 points as the minimum.

The following is a description of each part of the test as well as the point values for performances. A player can receive higher than 10 points in any phase of the test by exceeding the maximum performance standard.

Vertical jump

A strip of white tape is placed on the wall. It is perpendicular to the floor and six feet from the floor. It is

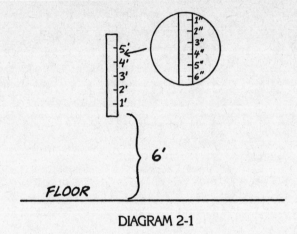

DIAGRAM 2-1

calibrated in inches and is five feet long (Diagram 2-1). The contestant stands up straight and reaches as high as possible with one arm, while both feet remain flatly on the floor. Once the point where his outstretched hand meets the tape is recorded, the distance used for scoring is the difference between that point and the highest point he touches while jumping. The player is allowed three jumps, all of which must start with one foot flat on the ground and touching the wall. This phase of the test measures the player's explosiveness. The point values are as follows:

33 in.— 10 pts.
31 in.— 9 pts.
29 in.— 8 pts.
27 in.— 7 pts.
25 in.— 6 pts.
23 in.— 5 pts.
22 in.— 4 pts.
21 in.— 3 pts.
19 in.— 2 pts.
17 in.— 1 pt.
Less than 16 in.— 0 pts.

(.5 points are awarded for each inch in
between or above the maximum performance)

40-yard dash

We attempt to find the fastest possible surface for this test. One coach stands at the start and one coach at the finish line. Only one player runs at a time. The coach at the starting line gives the starting command, but the other coach does not start the stop watch on this verbal signal. The watch is started on the first movement of the player. We believe this is a very accurate method of measuring the real speed of the athlete. We do not start the watch on the starting command because we feel some players will react to the command faster than others; therefore, reaction time will be involved rather than just speed. This phase of the test measures the athlete's quickness and explosiveness. The point values are as follows:

4.5 sec.— 10 pts.
4.7 sec.— 9 pts.
4.9 sec.— 8 pts.
5.1 sec.— 7 pts.
5.3 sec.— 6 pts.
5.5 sec.— 5 pts.
5.7 sec.— 4 pts.
5.9 sec.— 3 pts.
6.1 sec.— 2 pts.
6.3 sec.— 1 pt.
Over 6.4 sec.— 0 pts.

(.5 points are awarded for each .1 second in between or above the maximum performance)

Push-ups

These are done in very strict form. The coach counts for each player. We used to allow players to count for each other, but they were not nearly as demanding regarding strictness as the coach. A player is not allowed to rest once he begins, and his chest must touch the fist of the coach that is placed on the floor. This phase of the test measures the player's strength and endurance. The point values are as follows:

100 push-ups — 10 pts.
90 push-ups — 9 pts.
80 push-ups — 8 pts.
70 push-ups — 7 pts.
60 push-ups — 6 pts.
50 push-ups — 5 pts.
40 push-ups — 4 pts.
30 push-ups — 3 pts.
20 push-ups — 2 pts.
10 push-ups — 1 pt.
0 push-ups — 0 pts.

(.1 points are awarded for each push-up in between or above the maximum performance)

Side-stepping

Lines are placed on the gym floor, using 2½-inch tape. The lines are three feet long and placed four feet apart. The player begins by straddling one of the sidelines. From this point, he is given ten seconds to cross or touch as many lines as possible, while he keeps his body facing straight ahead. Like the 40-yard dash, time begins on the first movement of the player. One coach keeps track of the time while a second coach counts the lines that are touched or crossed (Diagram 2-2).

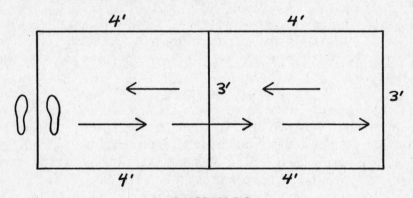

DIAGRAM 2-2

This phase of the test measures the athlete's quickness and agility. The point values are as follows:

30 lines— 10 pts.
28 lines— 9 pts.
26 lines— 8 pts.
24 lines— 7 pts.
22 lines— 6 pts.
20 lines— 5 pts.
18 lines— 4 pts.
16 lines— 3 pts.
14 lines— 2 pts.
12 lines— 1 pt.
Less than 11 lines— 1 pts.

(.5 points are awarded for each line in
between or above the maximum performance)

Mile and one-half run

This test is run on a quarter-mile track. Since the four
groups finish the first four events at the same time, the
entire team is together for this test. Each group completes
the run before the next group begins. This takes more time
than allowing the entire team to run together, but it allows
the members of each group to keep track of each other. It
makes the run very competitive, and it actually becomes a
race. This brings out the competitive spirit of each player.
The competitive spirit is also helped by the other members
of the squad who are on the sidelines cheering their
teammates. The coach calls out the time as each player
passes the starting line. This allows each athlete to know if
he is keeping up with the time he set for himself as a goal.
This phase of the test measures the player's endurance.
The point values are as follows:

9 min. and 30 sec.— 10 pts.
9 min. and 50 sec.— 9 pts.
10 min. and 10 sec.— 8 pts.
10 min. and 30 sec.— 7 pts.
10 min. and 50 sec.— 6 pts.
11 min. and 10 sec.— 5 pts.
11 min. and 30 sec.— 4 pts.
11 min. and 50 sec.— 3 pts.

12 min. and 10 sec.— 2 pts.
12 min. and 30 sec.— 1 pt.
Over 12 min. and 40 sec.— 0 pts.

(.1 points are awarded for each 2 seconds in between or above the maximum performance)

The scores are kept by each coach, and they are totaled after the fifth event. The scores are then posted in the locker room in an order from the highest to the lowest score in each group. Those players who did not achieve the minimum score are not given uniforms and told that they must watch practice. They are not allowed to participate until they pass the test.

POSITION DESCRIPTIONS

The following position descriptions contain the characteristics that we would like each defensive player to have. These are the characteristics we want. They are not necessarily the ones we always find. Even though we encourage the players to play certain positions, the final choice is their own. Using this method of personnel placement, it is very rare for a player to select a position for which he is unsuited. It is even more rare for a player to select a position that he was not encouraged to play by the coach.

Guards

This position does not require great size or speed, nor does it require great athletic ability. If we were to rate our starting defensive team's athletic ability from 1, the best athlete; to 11, the poorest athlete; the guards would normally be numbers 10 and 11. They must be very aggressive and have great desire, and these traits must compensate for their lack of athletic ability. We often put a sophomore or junior in this position, so he can develop both physically and mentally to be able to play the tackle position as a senior. We do expect the guards to have good upper-body strength, as they are often double-teamed and must be able to fight through it. Versus the pass, the offside guard is responsible for the middle screen and draw. He must have the ability to recognize these plays and have enough self-control to not overrush and be out of position to stop them. The following is the range of characteristics of athletes who have played the guard position:

Height 5'5"— 6'3"
Weight 160 lbs.— 205 lbs.
40-Yard Speed 5.0— 5.4

Tackles

Our biggest and best interior linemen play the tackle positions. They must have good athletic ability as they are responsible for the quarterback on the option when they are playing to the onside. They must also possess the discipline to play the quarterback, when he is their responsibility, and not attack the dive back. Since they "Slant" or play "Up" on the offensive tackle or tight end, who are normally the biggest and best blockers on the offense, the tackles must possess the size and strength to handle this responsibility. They need the quickness to cover the outside screen and the agility to "pop" the tight end to keep him from getting a quick pass release. When the onside tackle plays to the split-end side, he is often blocked by a lead back. He needs the ability to force the blocker into the hole and prevent a lane from opening in the defensive front. The following is the range of characteristics of the athletes who have played the tackle position:

Height 5'11"— 6'4"
Weight 185 lbs.— 205 lbs.
40-Yard Speed 4.8— 5.2

We use a very simple rule for the placement of the personnel in the interior line. We take our four best defensive linemen and put the biggest, strongest, and quickest at the tackles. The two that remain are placed at the guard positions. This method of placement has been very effective for us.

Ends

This position is filled by the most reckless members of the defensive squad. As they are playing the offside end, their responsibility is to get into the backfield and force something to happen. They must possess good quickness and a good deal of athletic ability. They are responsible for various pass coverages and, on occasion, must play man-to-man coverage on a back coming out of the backfield. There are times when they are responsible for the pitch on the option, and they must have the discipline to stay with the pitch and not attack the quarterback. Strength is a key to the end position. The offense often attempts to block the ends with pulling guards or lead backs; the ends must have the strength to defeat these blocks, or the great quickness to avoid the blocks, and be able to make the play.

In the two years we used the Combination-60, three of our four starting defensive ends made the All-League Team. Yet, none of them weighed more than 160 pounds. Our defensive ends have lead our team in quarterback sacks while being among the team leaders in interceptions. We have found this to be the ideal position for the "little tough guy" who has more pride and desire than size and plays the game with reckless abandonment. The following is the range of characteristics of the athletes who have played the end position:

Height 5'7"— 6'2"
Weight 156 lbs.— 205 lbs.
40-Yard Speed 4.8— 5.2

Linebackers

The athletes who play this position should possess many of the same qualities as the ends. They need very good quickness as they have a great deal of pass responsibility. There are situations when they are required to play a back or a tight end in man-to-man coverage. Other requirements are strength and endurance. Since the offense attempts to block the linebackers on every running play, and it is their responsibility to be the most active tacklers on the defensive unit, they must have the ability to play with this constant physical pressure. Unlike the ends, the linebackers are expected to make tackles from sideline to sideline. This responsibility requires good speed and excellent range. We expect these athletes to be in on 90 percent of all running play tackles, and the Combination-60 is geared to allow them to do this. The linebacker should be very aggressive but must play with a great deal of control.

The linebackers make the defensive calls for the front eight, both in the huddle and on the ball. In order to fulfill this responsibility, they need the intelligence to recognize the various offensive formations, and the ability to react to them. Linebackers must be respected and admired members of the defensive unit, since their verbal commands control the actions of the entire front. Leadership is a key to a linebacker's success. We have found that every year a linebacker has been elected by the defensive unit as a captain. This position of honor certainly shows the respect and admiration the members of the defensive team have had for the linebackers. The following is the range of characteristics of the athletes who have played the linebacker position:

Height 5'8"— 6'3"
Weight 165 lbs.— 200 lbs.
40-Yard Speed 4.8— 5.1

Halfbacks

They should be the fastest people on the defensive unit. They, like the safety, are called upon to cover large areas on zone coverages. Unlike the safety, they play man-to-man coverage against the fastest players on the opponent's team. The halfbacks must be strong tacklers. On most zone coverages they are responsible for any running plays that get outside the front contain. On man-to-man, if their key blocks, they have to force the run right away. There are many times when they are responsible for the pitch on the option, and this type of tackling takes a player with quick feet who will not be faked out of position in the open field. They must be physical players, because there are occasions when they have to defeat the block of a pulling tackle or guard to get to the ballcarrier. The halfbacks need the ability to recognize various offensive sets and to align properly against them. They also need excellent hands. The following is the range of characteristics of athletes who have played the halfback position:

Height 5'7"— 6'0"
Weight 145 lbs.— 175 lbs.
40-Yard Speed 4.5— 4.8

Safety

This is the most important position on the defense. He is the last line of defense between the opponent and the goal line. This position should be filled by the best athlete on the defensive unit. He must have excellent range, for he is called upon to cover large sections of the field on various zone coverages. His speed does not have to be great but he has to be able to cover a tight end or a running back in a man-to-man coverage. Since the safety is responsible for making secondary direction calls once the play begins, he must possess the ability to recognize various offensive keys and the intelligence to react quickly to them. Since his calls, in the huddle and on the open field, direct the other members of the secondary, he has to be a player who is respected by other members of the squad. Like the other members of the secondary, the safety must have good hands and be a very sure tackler. The following is the range of characteristics of athletes who have played the safety position:

Height 5'9"— 6'1"
Weight 150 lbs.— 185 lbs.
40-Yard Speed 4.6— 4.9

ALIGNMENT AND PLAY OF THE COMBINATION-60 INTERIOR LINE

3

Prior to a detailed analysis of the interior line play, it is important to understand certain concepts concerning the defense.

1. The defensive guard and the tackle to the side of the call are referred to as the *onside* linemen. The guard and the tackle to the side away from the call are referred to as the *offside* linemen. There are several reasons why this is important:
   a. The use of these terms helps make an explanation of the alignments and techniques clear and easily understood.
   b. The responsibilities of the offside tackle differ from those of the onside tackle.

2. The second important concept is the way the Combination-60 Defense divides the offensive line of scrimmage:
   a. The offensive line is split into segments.
   b. Each offensive lineman is divided into two segments; while each offensive gap that is four feet wide or less is also divided into two segments.
   c. Each segment is no more than two feet wide. When the gap between two offensive linemen

43

is greater than four feet, more than two segments exist. The importance of this wide split is explained when *Cheat Adjustment* is discussed later in the chapter.

d. Between each segment is an imaginary line called a midline. This midline is located down the middle of an offensive lineman and down the middle of an offensive gap that is no wider than four feet. These midlines are significant in the location of target points and for alignment purposes.

e. Target points occur where certain midlines intersect the line of scrimmage (Diagram 3-1).

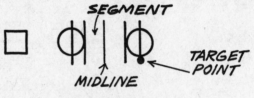

DIAGRAM 3-1

GUARDS

Stance

The guard uses a basic three-point stance. The shoulders are square and parallel to the line of scrimmage. The neck is "bulled" and the head is up with the eyes focused on the football. If the ball cannot be seen because of a deep alignment, the eyes are then focused on the down hand of the nearest offensive lineman. The feet are at least shoulder width apart. This varies according to the height of the player. A tall player may have his feet wider than shoulder width.

The right-handed player has his right arm down slightly in front of his shoulder and inside his right knee. His hand is open and weight is on the finger tips. The left arm is bent across the left thigh and ready to deliver a blow. The right foot is staggered and in a toe-instep relationship with the left foot. The opposite is true for the left-handed player.

The knees are flexed and bowed out slightly. The toes

are pointed a bit to the inside. The weight is distributed in a way that allows the player to move right, left, or straight ahead with ease and quickness. Most importantly, he never leans in any direction.

Alignment

The two basic alignments used by the guards are the "Slant" and "Up." The depth at which the guard aligns, while using these two alignments, is of prime importance. When "Slant" is being employed, the defender puts his down hand three and one-half feet from the near tip of the ball. The guard lines up as tight to the line of scrimmage as legally possible when "Up" is used.

"Slant"

The guard aligns with his nose on the midline of the offensive guard (Diagram 3-2).

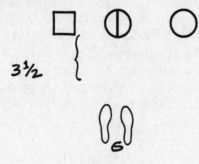

DIAGRAM 3-2

"Up"

The alignment is determined by the direction of the call. He aligns with his onside foot as tight to his "Slant" target point as possible. This target point is four segments to the onside of his original "Slant" alignment (Diagram 3-3).

Technique

"Slant"

The "Slant" is a four-step attack that is executed on a 45-degree angle toward the predetermined target point.

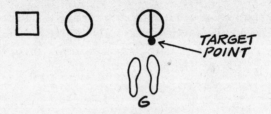

DIAGRAM 3-3

After a great deal of experimentation, it was decided that the first step of the "Slant" would be a crossover step with the offside foot, as opposed to a lead step with the onside foot. This first step is called the direction step, for it is directed to the target point. The second step is taken with the onside foot and is aimed two feet outside the target point. This allows the lineman to have a wide base. If contact is made at this point, the defender is in a strong position to fight through the block. The third step is aimed one foot inside the target point. On this step, contact is usually made with the offensive player to whom the defender is slanting. The fourth step is a natural follow step with the onside foot. It is used to square the defender with the line of scrimmage and to give him a sturdy base to fight any block. When the "Slant" is executed correctly, the onside foot is on the target point upon completion of the fourth step (Diagram 3-4).

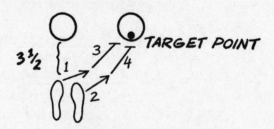

DIAGRAM 3-4 "Slant-Right"

The "Slant" is done in a good, low football position. The lineman strives to keep his shoulders parallel to the line of scrimmage during the entire attack. When contact is made with the offensive blocker, a two-hand shiver is delivered under the shoulder pads of the blocker. This keeps the lineman from getting "tied up" with the blocker and allows him to flow quickly to the ball. The most important aspect of the "Slant," and the point that is constantly stressed, is that the defender can never get cut off before reaching his target point. If the blocker meets him prior to reaching his target point, he must fight to keep his shoulders square and to get to his predetermined area. He fights through the block and never goes around it.

Once the defender reaches and controls his area, he is expected to make tackles on both sides of the target point. The defender is coached to get a piece of the offensive player to whom he is slanting. If the offensive player vacates the area before the defender gets to the target point, he then controls the area and gets to a depth of 1 yard in the backfield. During the entire "Slant," the defender searches for the ball as he fights through the pressure of any offensive player who attempts to block him (Diagram 3-5).

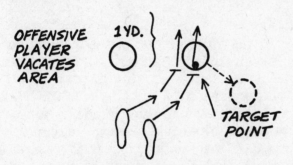

DIAGRAM 3-5 "Slant-Right"

There are some common mistakes that occur when an interior lineman uses the "Slant" technique. The following are some of the more common errors:

1. He stands up and does not stay in a good hitting position. This allows the blocker to get under the shoulder pads of the defender and take him out of the play.

2. He does not make contact with the offensive player to whom he is slanting. The blocker is then free to block the linebacker or cut off the pursuit of another defensive player.

3. On the second step of the "Slant," contact is made with the offensive player to whom he is slanting, and the defender does not fight through him, nor does he square himself to the line of scrimmage. This causes the defender to be cut off and a hole in the defensive front results (Diagram 3-6).

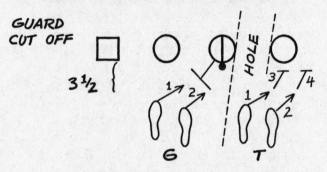

DIAGRAM 3-6 "Slant Right

"Up"

The "Up" is an extension of the "Slant." The interior lineman initially aligns with his onside foot on the target point rather than slanting to it. It is a two-step attack. The first step is taken with the foot closest to the midline of the offensive player on whom the defender is aligned. As the step is taken, a forearm shiver is delivered under the shoulder pads of the offensive player. The shiver is used to defeat the block of the opponent, while the free arm is working to shed him. The second step is taken with the opposite foot and is used to square the defender to the opponent and to the line of scrimmage. The defender fights through the pressure of the block if the offensive player attempts to block him. If the offensive player attempts to vacate the area, the defender must get a piece of him and control the area. Like "Slant," he is responsible for plays on both sides of the target point (Diagram 3-7).

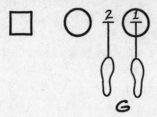

DIAGRAM 3-7 "Up-Right"

There are also some common errors made by the defensive lineman when he uses the "Up" technique. The following are some of them:

1. He does not fight through the pressure being applied by the blocker. The offensive player can then turn the defender away from the target point and eliminate him from the play.

2. The defender does not shed the blocker, and contact is maintained for too long a period of time. This wastes valuable time that the defender should be using to stop the offensive plays.

3. The defensive lineman allows himself to get too deep in the backfield. Overpenetration, such as getting cut off while slanting, creates a hole in the defense.

Keeping the shoulders parallel to the line of scrimmage has been emphasized throughout the description of the "Slant" and "Up" techniques. There are only three times that we allow the defender to turn his shoulders:

1. When the defender is sure the play is a pass, he has to turn his shoulders to get by the pass blocker.

2. When he is being double-teamed, the defender is coached to turn his shoulders perpendicular to the line of scrimmage and to split the two blockers.

3. When the defensive lineman pursues a play, he is expected to keep his shoulders parallel to the line of scrimmage to prevent any cut back. When this threat is gone, he may turn his shoulders and take the proper pursuit angle to the ball.

For simplicity sake, the "Slant" and "Up" are explained and diagramed in one direction. The other direction is simply a mirror image of the one being used. In our discussion, "Slant" and "Up" are explained to the right.

"Slant"

The right (onside) guard slants four segments to the right. His target point is on the midline between the fourth and fifth segment to his right or below the head of the offensive tackle.

The left (offside) guard slants the same amount of segments as the right, and his target point is below the head of the offensive center (Diagram 3-8).

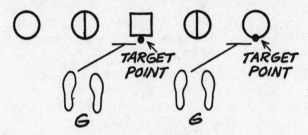

DIAGRAM 3-8 "Slant-Right"

"Up"

The right (onside) guard aligns with his onside foot on the target point below the offensive tackle.

The left (offside) guard aligns with his onside foot on the target point below the head of the offensive center (Diagram 3-9).

DIAGRAM 3-9 "Up-Right"

There are two alignment adjustments that are very important in executing the proper "Slant" and "Up" techniques. A serious problem arises when the slanting line-man is having difficulty getting a piece of the offensive player to whom he is slanting. The problems this causes have been explained earlier in this chapter. There are two alternatives that can be used to eliminate this problem. The lineman can use the "Up" technique rather than the "Slant." The second alternative, and the most commonly employed, is the *Cheat Adjustment.* This allows the slant-ing lineman to move one full segment to the onside and to execute the "Slant" from this alignment. The guard can cut his "Slant" to three segments (Diagram 3-10).

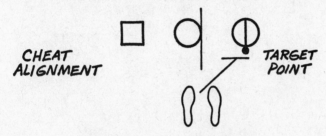

CHEAT ALIGNMENT   TARGET POINT

DIAGRAM 3-10 "Slant Right"

One weapon used by an offense to cause a problem for a slanting defensive lineman is to make the offensive line split wider than four feet or two segments. This causes the defensive lineman to use the *Wide Split Adjustment.* Since the "Slant" of the guard normally covers four segments, he merely adjusts his alignment so he still covers four seg-ments. When the right defensive guard is slanting to the right, and the split between the offensive guard and tackle is more than four feet or two segments, the defensive guard aligns so his "Slant" remains four segments. Rather than aligning with his nose on the midline of the offensive guard, he aligns at the point to the right of his normal alignment that allows him to slant four segments to his target point. The Wide Split Adjustment allows the defen-sive lineman to "Slant" the same amount of segments no matter how wide the splits are in the offensive line. When an excessively wide split occurs (wider than six feet) between the offensive interior linemen, which is very rare, the defensive lineman appears as though he is playing a gap technique. In reality, he is playing his normal "Slant" technique. Using the Wide Split Adjustment, rather than a gap charge technique, eliminates the possibility of over-penetration. It is also consistent with the normal "Slant" and does not create the need to teach a different gap charge technique (Diagram 3-11).

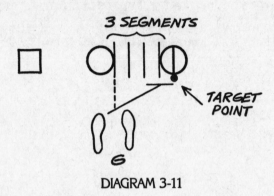

DIAGRAM 3-11

After the defense is called in the huddle, the interior linemen align in their normal "Slant" alignment on one knee. Being on one knee is a good position for the defenders to relax and catch their breath prior to the next play. When the offense breaks the huddle, the defenders put their down hand on the ground. As the offense reaches the line of scrimmage, the defenders assume their proper alignment and are ready to go. At this time, the interior line listens for the linebackers, who may make a *Defensive Call.* The defenders watch their key and attack as soon as the ball is snapped. If they cannot see the ball because of an alignment, they move on the movement of the down hand of the nearest offensive lineman.

Once the play begins, the defenders execute their techniques, then relentlessly pursue the ballcarrier until the whistle blows. *Pursuit* and *Gang Tackling* are the keys to successful defense. Proper pursuit angles and tackling techniques are covered in Chapter Ten.

Keys and Reactions

The use of the "Slant" and "Up" techniques has nearly eliminated the need for the interior defensive lineman to read the movement of the offensive line. However, there are certain offensive line keys that the defensive guard is expected to read.

When the defensive lineman reads a pass block, his reaction is to get to his target point, then rush the passer. The "Up" technique is best for a successful pass rush, but the "Slant" is also effective when the defender reacts quickly to the offensive lineman who shows pass.

When rushing the passer, there is one rule the defender always observes. He takes the shortest path to the quarterback and moves directly to him. He does not move laterally with the blocker but gets rid of him as quickly as possible. The methods used by the defensive lineman are determined by the actions of the pass blocker. The following are the methods employed:

1. When the blocker extends his elbow as a wing, the defender grabs the wing and attempts to turn the blocker perpendicular to the line of scrimmage.

2. When the blocker has too much weight on his heels as he drops back, the defender hits him high on the shoulder pads in an attempt to knock him over.

3. When the blocker lunges at the defender and puts his weight too far forward, the defender pulls him forward and down.

4. When the blocker tries to cut the rusher down at the knees, the defender forces the body of the blocker to the ground, while using a straight arm shiver to keep the blocker away from his legs.

5. When the blocker has good position and is in a strong stance to block, the defender fakes to one side of the offensive man and rushes to the other.

When the offside defensive guard "Slants" to the offensive center, he is aware of both the center and the offensive guard on whom he was originally aligned (offside offensive guard).

When the center steps toward the onside defensive guard, and the offside offensive guard makes a move to the offside, he reads this as a trap. The offside defensive guard is expected to execute his normal "Slant" and be prepared to fight through the trapping lineman. He is especially aware of keeping his shoulders parallel to the line and to not overpenetrate (Diagram 3-12).

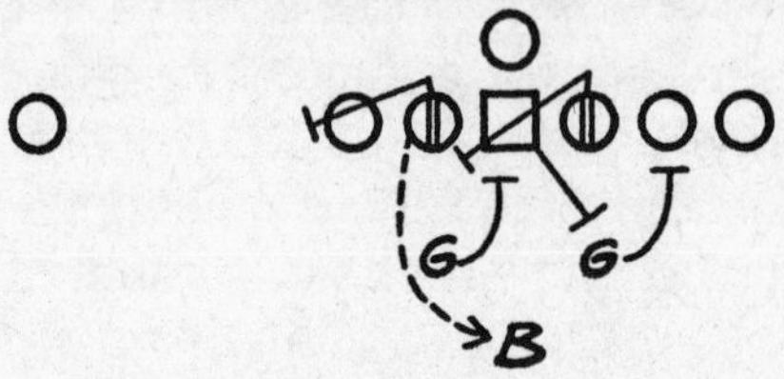

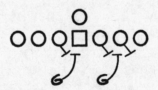

DIAGRAM 3-12 "Slant-Right"

When the defensive guard "Slants," he is aware of the offensive player to whom he is slanting and the offensive player on whom he was initially aligned. When both offensive players step in the same direction as the "Slant," the defender executes his normal "Slant" and is prepared to fight through the pressure of the offensive blocker on whom he was initially aligned. He strives to establish a stalemate so a hole does not develop in the defensive front (Diagram 3-13).

DIAGRAM 3-13 "Slant Right"

When a double-team block is used against the defensive guard, his responsibility is to split the blockers. Upon recognition of the double-team, he immediately drops to the knee that is closest to the point of attack. The defender turns his shoulders perpendicular to the line of scrimmage and shoots his hands and arms between the two blockers, while feverishly fighting to split the double-team. Even though his main objective is to tackle the ballcarrier, the defender is expected to at least create a pile at the point of offensive attack. He never allows himself to be pushed away from the play.

Run Responsibilities

The defensive guard is not given a particular responsibility against the run. He is expected to execute his proper technique and then get to the ballcarrier. He keeps his shoulders parallel to the line of scrimmage and pursues along the line until the threat of cutback has passed. He then gets into the proper pursuit angle and strives to make the tackle downfield.

Pass Responsibilities

The defensive guards do have particular responsibilities versus the pass. They, along with the offside defensive tackle, provide the inside pass rush. They attack the passer from the inside-out angle. The offside guard is responsible for the draw play and the middle screen. When the guards read outside screen, they continue to push the passer and force him to throw quickly (Diagram 3-26).

TACKLES

Stance

The defensive tackles use the same stance as the defensive guards.

Alignment

Like the defensive guards, the tackles use the "Slant" and "Up" alignments. They also use the same depth rules as the guards.

"Slant"

He aligns with his nose on the midline of the gap between the offensive tackle and the tight end (Diagram 3-14).

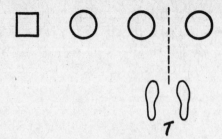

DIAGRAM 3-14

Versus a split end (any end split more than 2 yards from the offensive tackle), the onside tackle aligns as though the tight end is in his normal position, but he is as tight to the line of scrimmage as possible. This is called the *Split-End Rule*. The offside tackle assumes his normal slant alignment (Diagram 3-15).

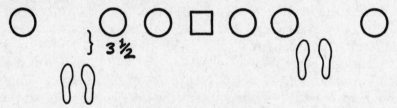

DIAGRAM 3-15 "Slant-Right"

A slot is treated in the same manner as an end. The only difference is that the onside tackle adjusts his depth so that he is aligned the same distance from the slot as he would have been from an end (Diagram 3-16).

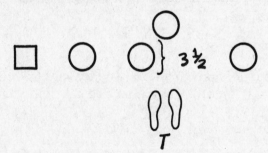

DIAGRAM 3-16 "Slant-Right"

DIAGRAM 3-17 "Up-Right"

"Up"

Like the guard, his alignment is also determined by the direction of the call. He aligns with his onside foot as tight to his "Slant" target point as possible. This target point is three segments to the onside of his original "Slant" alignment (Diagram 3-17).

Versus a split end, the onside tackle uses his Split-End Rule (Diagram 3-15). A split end has no effect on the offside tackle.

A slot is treated in the same manner as an end for both the onside and the offside tackles.

Techniques

The tackle uses the same techniques as the guard when he executes the "Slant" and "Up." The one difference is that the tackle "Slants" three segments and the guard "Slants" four. Like the defensive guard, the explanations and diagrams of the "Slant" and "Up" of the tackle are explained to the right.

"Slant"

The right (onside) tackle slants three segments to the right. His target point is on the midline between the third and fourth segment to his right or below the outside shoulder of the tight end (Diagram 3-18).

DIAGRAM 3-18 "Slant Right"

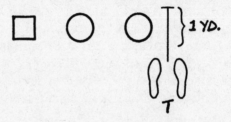

DIAGRAM 3-19 "Slant-Right"

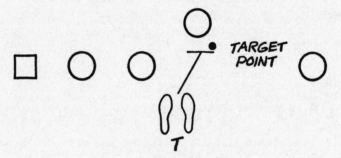

DIAGRAM 3-20 "Slant Right"

When the onside tackle is slanting to a split end, he uses the Split-End Rule and fires 1 yard into the backfield (Diagram 3-19).

When the onside tackle is slanting to a slot, he uses his Slot Alignment and "Slants" as though the slot is a tight end (Diagram 3-20).

The left (offside) tackle slants the same amount of segments as the right tackle, and his target point is below the onside shoulder of the offensive tackle (Diagram 3-18).

"Up"

The right (onside) tackle aligns with his onside foot on the target point below the tight end. Versus a split end or slot, he uses the special alignment rules that apply. The left tackle aligns with his onside foot on the target point below the onside shoulder of the offensive right tackle (Diagram 3-21).

DIAGRAM 3-21 "Up-Right"

The tackle also uses the Cheat Adjustment and the Wide Split Adjustment. The onside tackle is less concerned about the Wide Split Adjustment. When the tight end splits more than 2 yards, he uses the Split-End Rule rather than the Wide Split Adjustment.

After the defense is called in the huddle, the tackles perform in the same manner as the guards.

Keys and Reactions

Like the guard, the defensive tackle also has certain offensive line keys he is expected to read. He reads and reacts to the pass block and double-team in the same manner as the defensive guards.

When the onside defensive tackle is slanting, he is aware of the movement of the tight end. When the end attempts to release outside, the tackle strives to get a piece of him, then reacts inside to either option or pass. He does not step wider than the original target point as he attempts to hit the end. If he steps out too far, a hole develops in the defense and the option quarterback could turn up in it. If a dropback pass develops, he could be too far out of position to put on an effective pass rush (Diagram 3-22).

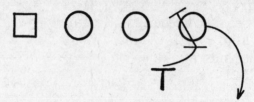

DIAGRAM 3-22 "Slant-Right"

When the offside tackle is slanting, he is aware of the tight end and offensive tackle. When both offensive players step in the same direction as the "Slant," he reacts in the same manner as the defensive guard (Diagram 3-23).

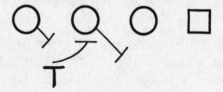

DIAGRAM 3-23 "Slant-Right"

When the onside tackle is using the "Up" technique and the tight end tries to release inside, he steps down with him and looks for a trapping guard or a blocking back coming at him (Diagram 3-24).

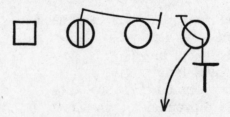

DIAGRAM 3-24 "Up-Right"

Run Responsibilities

The tackle has the same run responsibilities as the defensive guard. There is one exception. The onside tackle is responsible for the quarterback on the option play. He never allows the quarterback, with the football, to get outside of him. The tackle does not attack him until he turns up inside or comes to the target point. He is very conscious of keeping his shoulders parallel to the line of scrimmage. While playing the option in this "soft" manner, the tackle is in a very good position to play both the quarterback and the pitchman. When the pitch is made, prior to the quarterback reaching the target point, the tackle can then attack the pitchman. When this occurs, the tackle attacks from an inside-out angle (Diagram 3-25).

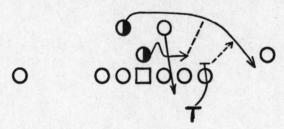

DIAGRAM 3-25

Pass Responsibilities

The offside tackle has the same responsibilities as the onside defensive guard. When he reads outside screen, he continues to attack the quarterback. The onside defensive tackle rushes the passer using an outside-in angle. He,

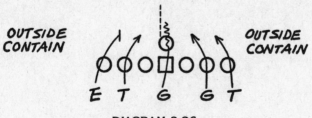

DIAGRAM 3-26

along with the offside defensive end, provides the outside pass rush. When he reads an outside screen pass to his side, he drops off the rush and attempts to get to the receiver. When he reads an outside screen pass to the opposite side, he continues the pass rush (Diagram 3-26).

COACHING THE COMBINATION-60 LINEBACKERS AND DEFENSIVE ENDS

4

The alignment and play of the linebackers and ends have many similarities, and for this reason, one chapter describes both positions. Like the defensive line, the linebacker and end to the side of the call are referred to as onside players and those away from the call are offside.

LINEBACKERS

Stance

The shoulders are square and parallel to the line of scrimmage. While facing straight ahead, the eyes are focused on the offensive key. The back is bent slightly at the waist, with the arms hanging straight down. The feet are at least shoulder width apart and they are parallel. The knees are slightly bent in a flexed position and the weight is on the balls of the feet. This is called a *breakdown* position.

Alignment

The basic alignment of the linebackers is the same on both the "Slant" and "Up." Their depth is determined by the down and distance, but in their basic alignment, the onside linebacker is 3 yards; and the offside linebacker, versus a tight receiver, is 1 yard from the near tip of the ball. Since the alignment of the linebackers could be a key for the offensive team to the direction of the "Slant" or "Up," they align with their nose on the midline of the offensive guards until the quarterback gets under the center. If, from the scouting report, it is determined that the quarterback uses a long cadence, the linebackers stay in their initial alignment for a longer period of time. When the ball is snapped, prior to the movement of the line-backers to their correct alignment, they immediately move to that position. This causes a great deal of confusion for the offensive blockers (Diagram 4-1).

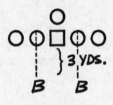

DIAGRAM 4-1

Onside Linebacker

He aligns with his nose on the midline of the center (Diagram 4-2).

Offside Linebacker

His alignment is determined by the type of offensive front that is employed to the offside of the defense.

Versus a tight end or slot (any end or slot who is split 2 yards or less from the offensive tackle), he aligns with his nose on the midline of that offensive player (Diagram 4-3).

Versus a flexed end or slot (any end or slot who is split more than 2 yards but less than 6 yards from the offensive

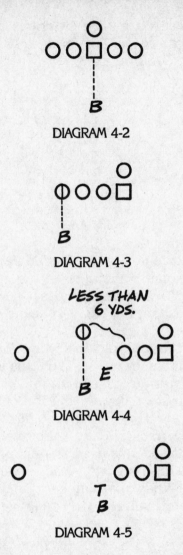

DIAGRAM 4-2

DIAGRAM 4-3

DIAGRAM 4-4

DIAGRAM 4-5

tackle), he also aligns with his nose on the midline of that offensive player (Diagram 4-4).

Versus a split end or slot (any end or slot who is split more than 6 yards from the offensive tackle), there are three alignments that can be employed. The first, and the one most often used, is the *Stack,* in which the linebacker aligns directly behind the defensive tackle (Diagram 4-5).

The second alignment is the *Walkaway.* He aligns 5

yards deep and 3 yards outside the offensive tackle. This is an excellent alignment to discourage the "Slant Pass" to the split receiver (Diagram 4-6).

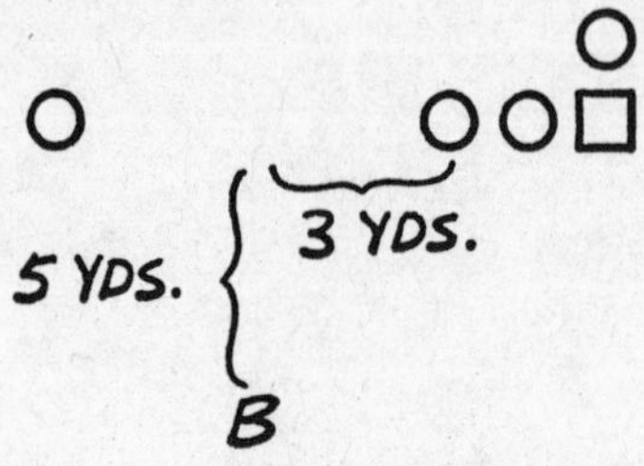

DIAGRAM 4-6

The third alignment is the *Double-Up.* He aligns with his nose on the inside shoulder of the split receiver, as tight to the line of scrimmage as possible. This alignment is not used very often. It weakens the defense, versus the run, to the offside (Diagram 4-7).

Versus a tight and split receiver to the same side, a Switch alignment can be used. When this is employed, the offside end assumes his normal alignment on the outside shoulder of the tight receiver. The linebacker moves to a Walkaway (splitting 3 yards from the tight receiver rather than the offensive tackle) or to a Double-Up on the split receiver. The Switch call is used as a change of pace. With the linebacker in the Walkaway, it is very effective against the run or pass. When the Double-Up is used in conjunction with the Switch call, it is very effective versus the pass (Diagram 4-8).

Keys and Reactions

Since a basic premise of the Combination-60 Defense is to keep the linebackers from getting blocked, the linebackers' reactions to the movements of their offensive line keys are different from those of most defenses. They read the head of the offensive player on whom they are aligned, then react to that movement. The reaction is a two-step

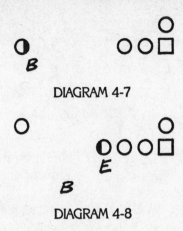

DIAGRAM 4-7

DIAGRAM 4-8

movement. The first step is up and in the direction the linebacker intends to go. The second step is a natural follow step. When the linebacker is going to the right, he first steps with his right foot, and vice versa. Upon completion of this movement, he either attacks the running play or assumes his pass coverage responsibility. When a blocker does get to the linebacker, he meets him in a good breakdown position, attacks the blocker with a forearm shiver, and sheds him with the free hand. Like the defensive lineman in an "Up" technique, the linebacker does not go around the blocker but through him to the play.

Onside Linebacker

There are only two blockers on the offensive front who can directly block the linebacker without first being attacked by another member of the defensive front. They are the offensive guards (Diagram 4-9). Another important point which the linebackers should keep in mind is that the onside G gap is the weakest gap along the defensive front.

There are several reasons why the onside G gap is the weakest along the line of scrimmage. When a "Slant" to the right or left is called, there is no defensive lineman initially aligned in the gap and no lineman passes through it while executing the slant. Even though the offside

DIAGRAM 4-9

defensive guard is responsible for the onside G gap, it is a difficult responsibility since he is slanting from an alignment on the offside offensive guard.

When an "Up" to the right or left is used, the offside defensive guard is still responsible for the onside G gap, but he is aligned to the offside of the center. The defensive guard could have some difficulty covering the onside G gap from this alignment.

When the head of the center comes straight ahead, the linebacker moves to the onside G gap. He knows that this gap is the one the offside defensive guard has the most difficulty protecting (Diagram 4-10).

DIAGRAM 4-10

When the head of the center goes down the line to either the onside or offside, the movement of the linebacker is in the direction the center is going. This is true when both the "Up" and "Slant" are used.

When the "Up" is used, this movement puts the linebacker in an excellent position to defend against the offensive blocking schemes that this movement of the center indicates. The following are the most common blocking schemes:

1. When the center steps down the line to the offside, it is an attempt to cut off the offside guard and keep

him from penetrating into the backfield. The linebacker is aware of the offside offensive guard who
may attempt to cutoff block him or pull to the
outside (Diagram 4-11).

DIAGRAM 4-11

2. When the center steps down the line to the onside, it
   indicates a type of Switch blocking between the
   center and the onside offensive guard. The center
   attempts to cut off the linebacker and the onside
   offensive guard comes inside to block the defensive
   guard (Diagram 4-12).

DIAGRAM 4-12

When the "Slant" is used, this movement of the linebacker also puts him in an excellent position to combat the
various zone blocking combinations that the center's
movement indicates. When zone blocking combinations
are used, the offensive linemen take their initial step in the
direction of the play and then block according to the
movements of the defense. The following are the most
common area blocking combination schemes:

1. When the center steps down the line to the offside, a
   Switch block between the center and offside offensive guard often occurs. The center attempts to pick
   up the offside guard, and the offensive guard attempts to take the linebacker (Diagram 4-13).
2. When the center steps down the line to the offside, a
   cross block between the center and the offside offen-

sive guard is a possibility. The center attempts to
pick up the linebacker, and the offensive guard
attempts to block the defensive guard (Diagram
4-14).

DIAGRAM 4-13

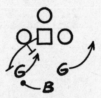

DIAGRAM 4-14

3. When the center steps down the line to the onside, a
   cutoff blocking situation can occur. The center
   attempts to pick up the linebacker, and the onside
   offensive guard attempts to cut off the "Slant" of the
   onside defensive guard (Diagram 4-15).

4. When the center steps down the line to the onside, a
   cross block between the center and the onside offensive guard may be attempted. The center tries to
   block the onside defensive guard and the onside
   offensive guard tries to pick up the linebacker
   (Diagram 4-16).

When the "Up" is used and the center blocks the
offside guard who is aligned on him, the linebacker's
movement is to the same side of the defensive guard as the
center's head. If the center's head goes offside, the linebacker's movement is to the offside and vice versa (Diagram 4-17).

When the "Slant" is used and the center's head goes
directly toward the onside or offside guard, the linebacker's movement is straight ahead. This movement puts

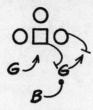

DIAGRAM 4-15

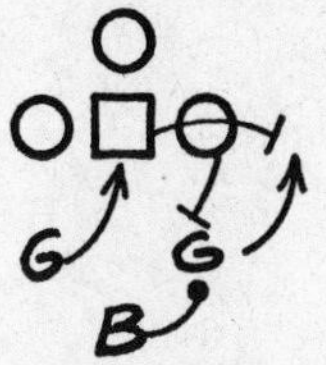

DIAGRAM 4-16

DIAGRAM 4-17

the linebacker in good position to combat the various blocking schemes that this center movement indicates. The following are the most common blocking schemes:

1. The center-guard fold block can occur when the center steps to either the onside or offside. The center attempts to block the defensive guard, and the offensive guard steps under the center and attempts to block the linebacker (Diagram 4-18).

2. When the center steps to either the onside or offside, a *Trap* block is a definite possibility. The center attempts to block the defensive guard, and the offensive guard, to the side the center steps, pulls and attempts to trap the other defensive guard. The other offensive guard attempts to block the linebacker (Diagram 4-19).

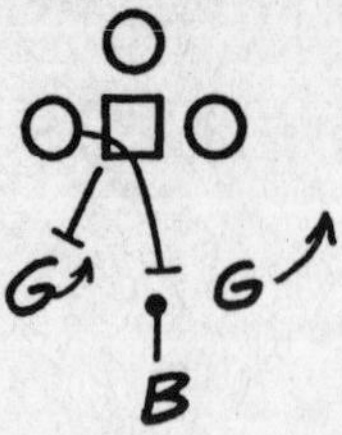

DIAGRAM 4-18

DIAGRAM 4-19

3. When the center steps to the offside, an *Isolation* block is possible. The center attempts to block the offside defensive guard as the onside offensive guard attempts to block the onside defensive guard. A back attempts to pick up the linbacker (Diagram 4-20).

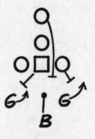

DIAGRAM 4-20

When the center shows pass, the movement of the linebacker is controlled by the action taken by the quarterback. As he moves to his pass coverage responsibility, he is aware of the *Draw* and the *Middle Screen* (Diagram 4-21).

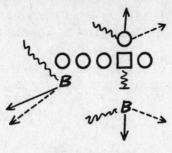

DIAGRAM 4-21

Offside Linebacker

The keys and reactions of the offside linebacker are determined by the type of offensive front that is employed to the offside of the defense.

Versus a tight end or slot, he reads the block of that offensive player. Even though the offside linebacker is responsible for outside contain versus the run; against a tight receiver, he has help from the defensive end who is aligned outside of him. This gives him more flexibility to play the off-tackle hole. The following are the reactions versus a tight receiver:

1. When the blocker comes directly at the linebacker, he steps up and uses the same attack technique as the onside linebacker. He fights though the block and always keeps outside leverage (Diagram 4-22).

DIAGRAM 4-22

2. When the blocker goes to either the onside or offside, the movement of the linebacker is in the same direction as the offensive player. He gets a piece of the player to keep him from a quick pass

release, or to keep him from blocking the defensive end or the onside linebacker (Diagram 4-23).

3. When the tight receiver shows pass, either by pass blocking or releasing on a pattern, the offside linebacker's pass responsibility is also controlled by the action taken by the quarterback and the coverage that is being used (Diagram 4-21).

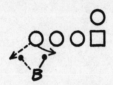

DIAGRAM 4-23

Versus a flexed end, the keys and reactions are the same as those versus a tight end or slot. The one difference is that the linebacker does not have a defensive end outside to help him with outside contain (Diagram 4-4).

When the Stack or the Walkaway is used, the line-backer's movement is to the onside. From that position, he locates the ball and attacks the running play or goes to his pass coverage responsibility (Diagram 4-24).

When the Double-Up is used, the linebacker steps into the receiver with his outside foot and attacks him. He sees into the formation with peripheral vision and reacts to the play (Diagram 4-25).

Blitz Techniques

The linebackers rarely blitz, but when they do, there are certain rules they follow:

1. They never start until the ball is snapped.
2. They attack a *gap*, not a man.
3. They shoot their arms through the gap in an effort to make themselves as "skinny" as possible to fit through the line opening.

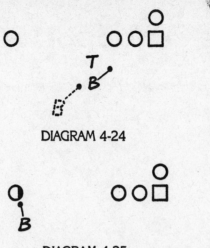

DIAGRAM 4-24

DIAGRAM 4-25

4. As they are moving, they analyze the play and keep control of their movement in order to make the play.

5. If they read screen, they continue to attack the quarterback. The screen is covered by the other members of the defense.

Run Responsibilities

Onside Linebacker

He is responsible for all plays in the G, T, and E gaps, but must attack all plays from sideline to sideline (Diagram 4-26). Since the defense is geared toward keeping the linebackers free from blockers, the onside linebacker must read only the block of the center and is then free to roam along the line of scrimmage. When a wide play is run (outside the E gap) and a seam develops along the line, it is his responsibility to shoot the seam and to tackle the play for a loss. If there is no seam, he gets into the proper pursuit angle and attacks the play from the inside-out (Diagram 4-27).

Versus the option, the linebacker is responsible for the ball. At first, we gave the onside linebacker dive

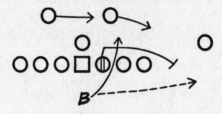

DIAGRAM 4-26

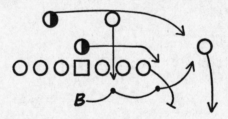

DIAGRAM 4-27

responsibility, but we found that he was attacking the dive back even when he did not have the ball. We then instructed him to attack the ball, rather than a specific phase of the option. The linebacker checks the dive back first, then the quarterback, and finally the pitchman. His basic responsibility is still the dive back, but he has the flexibility to read the play and attack the ballcarrier (Diagram 4-28).

DIAGRAM 4-28

Offside Linebacker

He is responsible for outside contain to the offside. He never allows any ballcarrier to get outside of him. When a play is run away from him, he gets into the proper pursuit angle to attack the play and stop it for a short gain (Diagram 4-29).

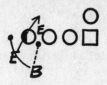

DIAGRAM 4-29

Versus the option, the linebacker is responsible for the pitchman when man-to-man, Stay, or Free Safety coverage is used (Diagram 4-30).

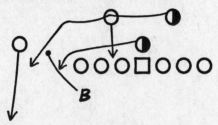

DIAGRAM 4-30

When Corner or Invert secondary coverage is employed, either a defensive halfback or the safety could cover the pitch. The offside linebacker could be given the quarterback or the dive back on the outside veer. In other words, he can be used to double cover any phase of the option. This is covered in greater detail in Chapter Eight.

Pass Responsibilities

The linebackers' pass responsibilities vary with the coverage that is employed. There are three basic types of coverage used: zone, man-to-man, and goal line. The responsibilities for zone and man-to-man are covered in this chapter, and the goal line is covered in Chapter Seven.

Onside Linebacker

On all zone coverages, the pass coverage responsibilities of the onside linebacker are the same and are based on the reactions of the linebacker to the various actions of the quarterback:

1. When the quarterback uses a passing action between the outside legs of the offensive guards, the linebacker drops back and favors the tight end side. He drops to a maximum depth of 12 yards. While he is dropping, he watches the quarterback, and with peripheral vision sees any receiver in his zone. His responsibility is the hook area (Diagram 4-31).

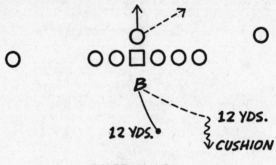

DIAGRAM 4-31

2. When the quarterback uses a passing action that is wider than the offensive guard, the linebacker sprints to the same side and covers the hook area to that side. He sprints to a maximum depth of 12 yards. If the ball is not thrown by the time he reaches his proper depth and there are no receivers in his zone, he drops back to help in the deep areas. As on dropback, the linebacker watches the quarterback and is aware of all receivers in his zone (Diagram 4-31).

When man-to-man coverage is used, the onside linebacker uses his normal zone coverage rule unless two backs go out of the backfield to one side. He plays the second back man-to-man (Diagram 4-32).

Offside Linebacker

Unlike the onside linebacker, his pass coverage responsibilities vary with the zone coverage that is called.

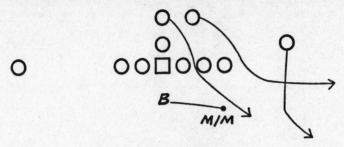

DIAGRAM 4-32

Like the onside linebacker, his reactions to pass are based on the movements of the quarterback. The following are the reactions of the linebacker to various actions of the quarterback when different zone coverages are employed:

1. When *Stay* is used, the linebacker's responsibility does not vary according to the passing action used by the quarterback. When the linebacker reads pass, he sprints to the flat area while watching the quarterback and looking for a back out of the backfield to his side. When a back comes out, he plays him man-to-man. When there is no back out of the backfield to his side, he then begins to drop straight back from the flat area. The linebacker looks for the wide receiver to his side. When the wide receiver runs any inside pattern under 15 yards, he picks him up man-to-man. When there is no inside route or no wide receiver, the linebacker drops to 15 yards then continues into his cushion on dropback. On action away, after reaching 15 yards, he sprints to help in the deep middle (Diagram 4-33).

2. When *Corner* or *Invert* is used, and the quarterback uses a passing action between the outside legs of the offensive guards or wider than the far offensive guard, his responsibility is the same as Stay. When the quarterback uses a passing action wider than the near offensive guard, the linebacker attacks him (Diagram 4-34).

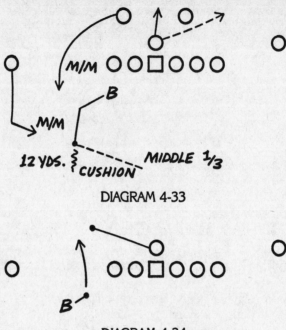

DIAGRAM 4-33

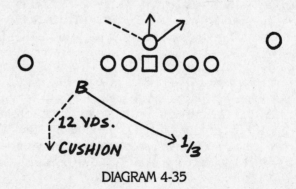

DIAGRAM 4-34

3. When *Free Safety* is used and the quarterback uses
   a passing action between the outside legs of the
   offensive guards or wider than the far offensive
   guard, the linebacker sprints to the deep middle
   one-third of the field. When the quarterback uses a
   passing action wider than the near offensive guard,
   he covers the flat area to his side, then the cushion.
   When this coverage is employed, the linebacker
   uses the Walkaway alignment (Diagram 4-35).

DIAGRAM 4-35

The basic man-to-man coverage rule for the onside linebacker is that he is responsible for the first back out of the backfield to the offside of the formation.

DEFENSIVE ENDS

Stance

The shoulders are square and parallel to the line of scrimmage. The head is facing inside with the eyes focused on the ball. The back is bent slightly at the waist with the arms hanging straight down. The inside foot is up with the toes of the back foot aligned at the heel of the up foot. The feet are shoulder width apart and the knees are slightly bent in a flexed position.

Alignment

The basic alignment of the ends is the same on both the "Slant" and "Up." They align with their inside foot as tight to the line of scrimmage as possible. Unless an "Up" technique is being used by the interior defensive line, they are the only defensive personnel on the line of scrimmage.

Onside End

His alignment is determined by the type of offensive front that is employed to the onside of the defense.

Versus a tight end or slot (any end or slot who is split 2 yards or less from the offensive tackle), he aligns 1 yard outside the offensive player. This 1-yard distance is from the outside foot of the offensive player to the inside foot of the defensive end (Diagram 4-36).

Versus a flexed end or slot (any end or slot who is split more than 2 yards but less than 6 yards from the offensive tackle), he aligns with his nose on the midline of that offensive player and employs the basic linebacker stance (Diagram 4-4).

Versus a split end or slot (any end or slot who is split more than 6 yards from the offensive tackle), there are three alignments that can be employed. The first is the *Stack*. The end aligns behind the onside defensive tackle (Diagram 4-5). The second is the *Walkaway*. He aligns 5 yards deep and 3 yards outside the offensive tackle (Diagram 4-6). The third alignment is the *Double-Up*. He aligns with his nose on the inside shoulder of the split receiver, as tight to the line of scrimmage as possible (Diagram 4-7). In all three alignments, the end employs the same stance as a linebacker.

Versus a flexed end or slot and a split end or slot, the onside end uses the same alignments as the offside linebacker.

Versus a wing (a back who is aligned less than 4 yards outside the tight end), he aligns with his nose on the outside shoulder of that offensive player in his basic end stance (Diagram 4-37).

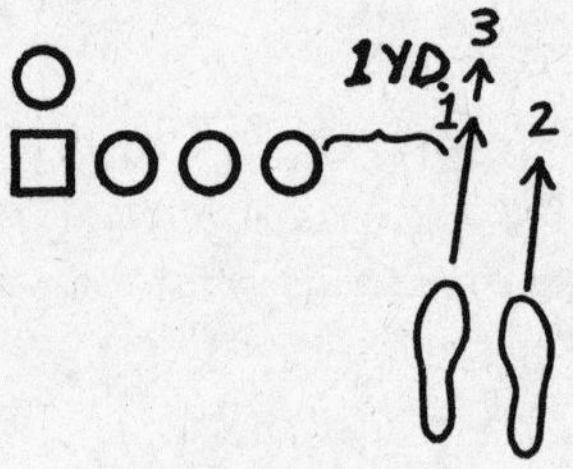

DIAGRAM 4-36

DIAGRAM 4-37

Offside End

Like the onside end, his alignment is also determined by the offensive front that is employed to the offside of the defense.

Versus a tight end or slot, he aligns his nose on the outside shoulder of that offensive player (Diagram 4-38).

DIAGRAM 4-38

Versus an end or slot who is split more than 2 yards, he aligns his inside foot 1 yard from the outside foot of the offensive tackle (Diagram 4-39).

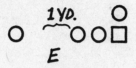

DIAGRAM 4-39

Versus a wing, he aligns on the tight end and disregards the wing.

Versus a tight receiver and split receiver to the same side, a Switch alignment can be used. This is described earlier in this chapter (Diagram 4-8).

Keys and Reactions

Like the offside linebacker, the keys and reactions of the ends are determined by the offensive front to their side.

Onside End

The keys and reactions of this position, versus certain offensive fronts, are the same as those of the offside linebacker. Versus a tight end or slot, he takes a three-step shuffle directly across the line of scrimmage on the snap of the ball. The shuffle is taken with the inside, outside, and inside foot. Upon completion of this shuffle technique, he is 1-yard deep in the backfield. From this point, he looks to the inside for any oncoming blockers, while watching the movements of the backs (Diagram 4-36). The following are his reactions to various blocking patterns:

1. When a blocker comes from the inside, he attacks the blocker and squeezes the play inside. He is very careful to keep outside leverage and his shoulders parallel to the line of scrimmage (Diagram 4-40).

DIAGRAM 4-40

2. When a back shows pass, the movement of the end is controlled by the action of the quarterback and by the coverage that is being employed (Diagram 4-41).

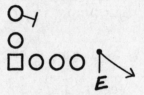

DIAGRAM 4-41

3. When no blocker attacks the end or no back shows pass, he holds his position until he reads the play and then reacts accordingly.

Versus a wing, he takes his shuffle through the wing and then reacts accordingly. It is very important that he keeps the wing from blocking the onside linebacker (Diagram 4-42).

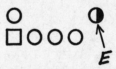

DIAGRAM 4-42

Versus a flexed end or slot and a split end or slot, he uses the same keys and reactions that the offside linebacker employs against these types of offensive fronts.

Offside End

His key is the football. On the snap, the offside end initiates his attack. He fires toward a point 1 yard in front of the near offensive set back. If he fires to a point deeper than this, there is a good possibility the play could be run inside of him. He would then find himself totally out of position to disrupt the offense (Diagram 4-43). It is very important that he keeps himself under control, so he can react to and stop the offensive play.

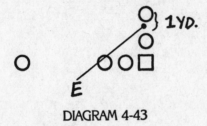

DIAGRAM 4-43

Versus a tight end or slot, he executes a *Pinch* as he fires into the backfield. The Pinch is a technique that requires the end to fire through the tight end or slot, as he moves into the backfield. The purpose of this technique is twofold. It keeps the receiver from a quick release to the outside, and it protects the linebackers from a block by this offensive player (Diagram 4-44).

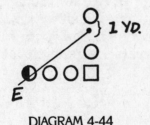

DIAGRAM 4-44

Versus a flexed end or slot and a split end or slot, he executes his basic fire technique (Diagram 4-43).

Run Responsibilities

Onside End

His responsibilities are the same as the offside line-backer against all offensive fronts except the tight end or slot. Unlike the offside linebacker, he has no defensive front player outside of him, so he must pay greater attention to outside contain and not concern himself with helping the onside linebacker with the E gap. When the play goes away, he trails on a flat path looking for the countertrap. He then gets as deep as the deepest back, looking for the reverse. When the reverse threat is gone he takes a good pursuit angle. (Diagram 4-45)

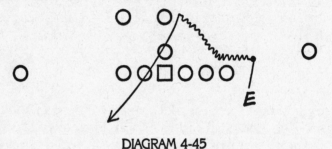

DIAGRAM 4-45

Offside End

His responsibility is to get into the offensive backfield and disrupt the play before it has a chance to fully develop. When action goes away, he slow trails, looking for any reverse or counteraction at the depth of the deepest back. Once all reverse threats are gone, he takes a good pursuit angle (Diagram 4-46).

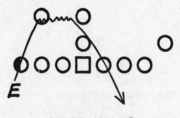

DIAGRAM 4-46

Versus the option, he is responsible for the quarterback. He attempts to get to the quarterback-running back mesh point. In this way, he not only disrupts that phase of the option, but he may also force a premature pitch.

Pass Responsibilities

Onside End

His responsibilities are the same as the offside linebacker, except his responsibilities are to the onside rather than the offside.

Offside End

His responsibility is to get to the quarterback. He provides the offside-outside pass rush. Like the defensive linemen, he takes the shortest path to the quarterback and moves directly to him. When he reads an outside screen pass to his side, he drops off the rush and attempts to get

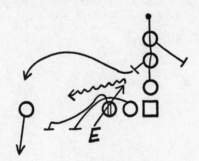

DIAGRAM 4-47

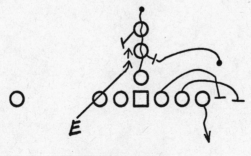

DIAGRAM 4-48

to the receiver, or at least force the quarterback to throw over him. (Diagram 4-47). When he reads an outside screen pass to the opposite, he continues the pass rush (Diagram 4-48).

ALIGNMENT AND PLAY OF THE COMBINATION-60 SECONDARY

5

Unlike the defensive front, the use of either "Slant" or "Up" has no effect on the alignment and play of the secondary. For this reason, the terms *onside* and *offside* are not used in the secondary.

HALFBACK

Stance

The halfback uses the same basic breakdown stance used by the linebackers. He keeps his inside foot back and the toes of the inside foot are aligned with the heel of the outside foot.

Alignment

In all coverages except Gap and Tough (covered in Chapter Seven), the halfbacks align at a 45-degree angle, facing the quarterback. In this alignment, they see the quarterback, and with peripheral vision, keep all potential receivers in sight (Diagram 5-1). Their basic depth is 7 yards. They align according to the widest receiver to their side of the offensive formation.

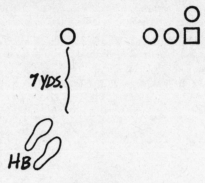

DIAGRAM 5-1

Versus a receiver who splits less than 10 yards from the offensive tackle, the halfback aligns 2 yards outside the receiver (Diagram 5-2).

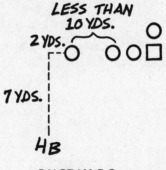

DIAGRAM 5-2

Versus a receiver who splits at least 10 yards but less than 13 yards, he aligns 1 yard outside the receiver (Diagram 5-3).

Versus a receiver who splits 13 or more yards, he aligns with his nose on the outside shoulder of the receiver (Diagram 5-4).

The halfback also has a sideline rule. He never aligns closer than 7 yards to the sideline. When a receiver aligns 7 yards or closer to the sideline, the halfback no longer aligns at a 45-degree angle. He aligns with his shoulders

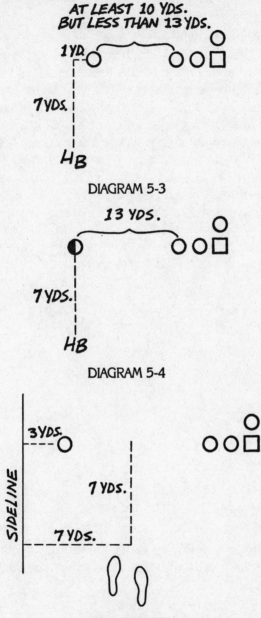

AT LEAST 10 YDS.
BUT LESS THAN 13 YDS.

1 YD.

7 YDS.

HB

DIAGRAM 5-3

13 YDS.

7 YDS.

HB

DIAGRAM 5-4

3 YDS.

SIDELINE

7 YDS.

7 YDS.

DIAGRAM 5-5

parallel to the line of scrimmage at a point 7 yards from the sideline. This alignment allows him to see the quarterback and, with peripheral vision, also see the receiver (Diagram 5-5).

Keys and Reactions

When zone coverages are used, the primary key of the halfback is the quarterback. While he is keying the quarterback, he is also aware of the movements of the receiver outside of whom he is aligned. His reactions are based on the movements of both offensive players. When man-to-man coverage is employed, he looks to his man as the primary key and is also aware of the movements of the quarterback. Aligning at a 45-degree angle gives him the opportunity to see the quarterback as well as the receivers.

The first reaction of the halfback is the same for both zone and man-to-man coverage. He uses a three-step shuffle that takes him straight back. The shuffle is taken with the inside, outside, and inside foot (Diagram 5-6). This gives him the time needed to read and react properly to his keys.

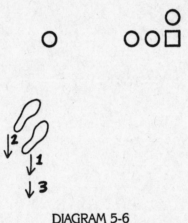

DIAGRAM 5-6

When man-to-man coverage is employed, the defensive halfback reacts in the following manners to the movements of his key:

1. When the key releases for a pass, he stays with his man and keeps a 2-yard cushion between himself and the receiver (Diagram 5-7).

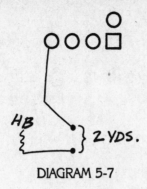

DIAGRAM 5-7

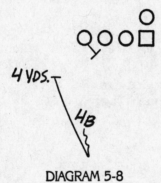

DIAGRAM 5-8

2. When the key blocks inside, he reacts to run and levels at 4 yards (Diagram 5-8).

3. When the key *Stalk* blocks the defensive halfback, he stays with him until the pass threat is gone or until the ball crosses the line of scrimmage (Diagram 5-9).

The reactions of the defensive halfback to the movements of the quarterback are determined by the zone coverage that is being used.

When the quarterback uses a passing action toward the defensive halfback that is wider than the near offensive guard, he reacts in the following manners:

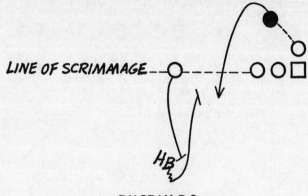

DIAGRAM 5-9

1. *Corner*—He levels at 7 yards, which is the flat zone (Diagram 5-10).
2. *Invert, Stay,* and *Free Safety*—He drops to the deep one-third zone (Diagram 5-11).

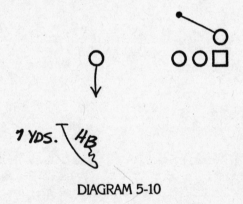

DIAGRAM 5-10

When the quarterback uses a passing action away from the defensive halfback that is wider than the far offensive guard, he reacts in the following manners:

1. *Corner* and *Invert*—He reacts to the deep two-third zone (Diagram 5-12).
2. *Stay, Free Safety*—He drops to the deep one-third zone (Diagram 5-13).

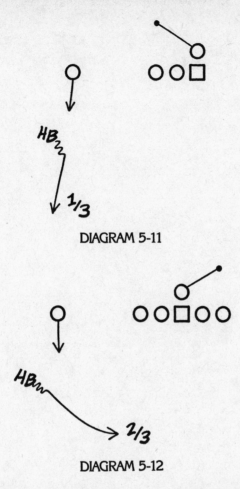

DIAGRAM 5-11

DIAGRAM 5-12

When the quarterback uses a passing action between the outside legs of the offensive guards, this is read as a dropback pass and he reacts in the following manner:

All zone coverages—He reacts to the deep one-third zone (Diagram 5-14).

When the quarterback either gives or runs the ball to the side of the defensive halfback, and the defensive halfback is sure the threat of pass is gone, he reacts in the following manner:

All zone coverages—He levels at 4 yards and keeps outside leverage on the ball (Diagram 5-15).

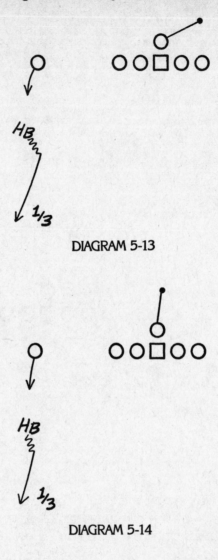

DIAGRAM 5-13

DIAGRAM 5-14

When the quarterback either gives or runs the ball away from the defensive halfback, and the defensive halfback is sure the threat of pass is gone, he reacts in the following manner:

All zone coverages—He reacts through the deep two-third zone, maintaining the proper pursuit angle on the play (Diagram 5-16).

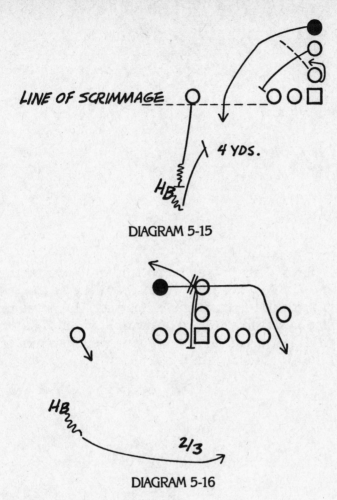

LINE OF SCRIMMAGE

4 YDS.

HB

DIAGRAM 5-15

2/3

HB

DIAGRAM 5-16

Run Responsibilities

The defensive halfback's responsibilities versus the run depend on the side of the formation to which the ball is run. When the ball is run to the side of the defensive halfback, he is the outside contain man. He can never allow the ball to get outside of him. He attacks the play from the outside-in. His job is to force all plays back into the pursuit (Diagram 5-17).

When the ball is run away from the defensive half-back, his responsibility is to stop the cutback run and any

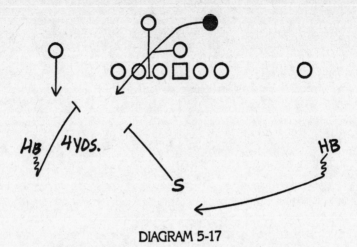

DIAGRAM 5-17

reverse plays. This is true in both man-to-man and zone coverage. He flows through the secondary at the proper pursuit angle to intersect the ballcarrier. He moves under controlled speed so as not to overrun any play. His rule is never to allow the ballcarrier to get deeper than him or cut back under him (Diagram 5-18).

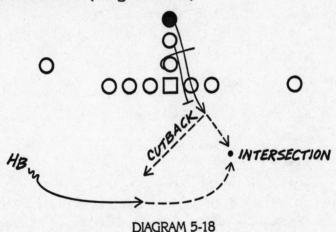

DIAGRAM 5-18

Versus the option, the responsibilities of the defensive halfback vary according to the coverage that is being employed and the side to which the option is run.

When the option is run to the side of the defensive halfback, his responsibilities are as follows:

Corner—His first responsibility is to check the flat zone. When he is sure it is a run, he levels to 4 yards and is responsible for the pitchman (Diagram 5-19).

All other zone coverages—His first responsibility is to cover any threat in his deep one-third zone. When the ball crosses the line of scrimmage, he levels to 4 yards and is responsible for the pitchman (Diagram 5-20).

Man-to-man—He stays with his man until the ball crosses the line of scrimmage. He then levels at 4 yards and is responsible for the pitchman (Diagram 5-21).

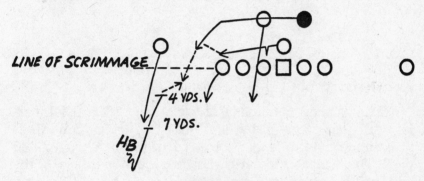

DIAGRAM 5-19

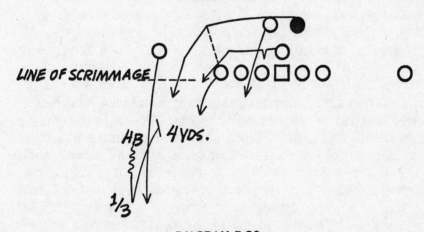

DIAGRAM 5-20

When the option is run to the side away from the defensive halfback, his normal run responsibilities apply.

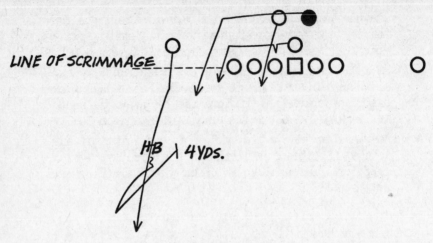

LINE OF SCRIMMAGE

HB 4 YDS.

DIAGRAM 5-21

Pass Responsibilities

The pass responsibility of the defensive halfback varies with the coverage that is used. One responsibility that remains constant is his job of preventing a completed pass. The best way to perform this duty is to intercept the ball, which is the goal of all defensive backs. When an attempt to intercept is impossible or when an unsuccessful attempt could lead to an offensive completion, the defender has two alternatives. When possible, he may knock the ball down. Or, when the interception or the knock down seem unlikely, he may strip the ball from the receiver upon completion of the pass.

When man-to-man coverage is employed, the defensive halfback's responsibility is to cover the first receiver to his side of the field. The defender plays on the receiver's outside shoulder. This position allows the defender to look through the receiver to the quarterback and to see the ball being released. Once the ball is thrown, the defender is in a position to play through the receiver to the ball. It also allows the defender to play the ball rather than the receiver. The defensive halfback is very careful not to step in front of the receiver too quickly in an attempt to intercept or knock down the ball. This could result in getting beat deep—the greatest error a defensive back can make.

The defensive back plays 2 yards deeper than the receiver. This cushion helps prevent the possibility of getting beat deep, while still being in a good position to step up and intercept or knock the ball down. When a receiver has exceptional speed, the defender may use a 3-yard cushion, but he cannot get to a distance where he is too far away from the receiver to step up and prevent the completion (Diagram 5-22).

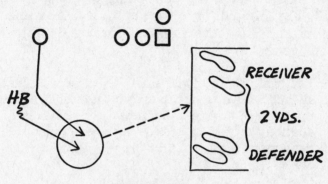

DIAGRAM 5-22

When zone coverage is used, the defender's first responsibility is to read the action of the quarterback. This action determines the zone he is to cover. Once he reads his key, he sprints to his zone, keeping all potential receivers between himself and the quarterback. He covers the deepest receiver in his zone as though man-to-man coverage is being used. He covers him until he leaves his zone or until the ball is thrown to another receiver. When the receiver leaves his zone, the defensive halfback calls to the defender in the next zone to alert him to the oncoming receiver. He is also aware of any receiver coming into his zone from another zone.

SAFETY

Stance

The safety uses the same basic breakdown stance that is used by the linebacker. When a zone coverage is used, he keeps his feet parallel rather than staggered. This allows him to open step to either the right or left, depending on the flow of the football. When man-to-man coverage is used, he uses the same stance as the defensive halfback.

Alignment

Unlike the defensive halfback, the depth and alignment of the safety vary according to the coverage that is used. The following are the depths and alignments when Corner and Stay coverages are employed against various offensive sets:

> The basic depth of the safety is 12 yards. His basic alignment is no wider than over the offensive guard to the wide of the field. He never allows himself to be aligned closer than 2 yards to the open-field side of a hash mark (Diagram 5-23).

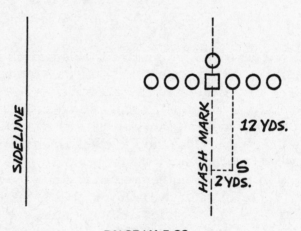

DIAGRAM 5-23

> Versus a formation with one wide receiver, the safety's depth is as deep as the wide receiver is wide. He aligns over the offensive guard to the same side as the wide receiver (Diagram 5-24).

> Versus a formation with a wide receiver to both sides, the safety's depth is 2 yards deeper than the widest

receiver is wide. He aligns over the guard to the side of the widest receiver. When both receivers are split approximately the same distance, he uses his basic alignment rule (Diagram 5-25).

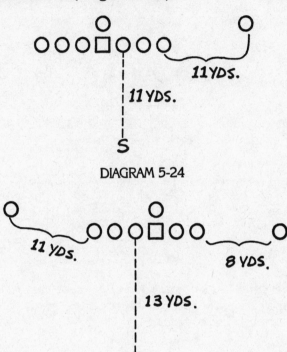

DIAGRAM 5-24

DIAGRAM 5-25

When Invert coverage is used, the safety uses the same alignments as Corner coverage, but he does not use the same depth rules. His depth is 7 yards. He moves to that depth from his normal 12-yard depth, prior to the snap of the ball. This helps to disguise the Invert coverage (Diagram 5-26).

When Free Safety is used, the safety begins at his basic depth and alignment, then moves to a different depth and alignment prior to the snap of the ball. When this coverage is called, the safety may have many different responsibilities, and these determine his alignment and depth. The following are the responsibilities he may be given and the depth and alignment he uses for them:

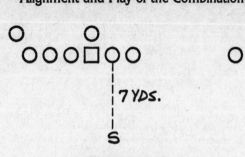

DIAGRAM 5-26

1. *Blitz.* He uses the same depth as a linebacker and his alignment is determined by the area into which he is to blitz (Diagram 5-27).

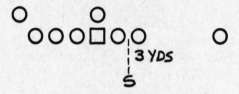

DIAGRAM 5-27

2. *Prevent.* He uses his basic alignment rule but his depth is between 15 and 25 yards, depending on the situation (Diagram 5-28).

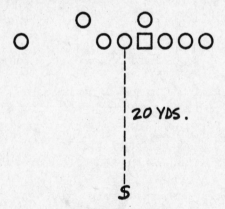

DIAGRAM 5-28

3. *Lock On.* He aligns on the outside shoulder of the receiver he is to cover. He aligns as tight to the receiver as possible (Diagram 5-29).

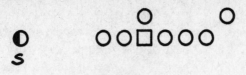

DIAGRAM 5-29

4. *Normal*. He uses his basic depth and alignment.

When man-to-man coverage is used, he aligns on the outside shoulder of the inside receiver to the twin receiver side. He uses the same 7-yard depth as the defensive halfback (Diagram 5-30).

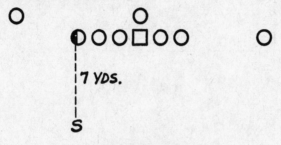

DIAGRAM 5-30

When an offensive team aligns with only one receiver to each side (three running backs remain in the offensive backfield), he aligns at his normal depth and alignment (Diagram 5-31).

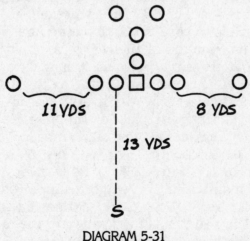

DIAGRAM 5-31

When an offensive team aligns with twin receivers on both sides, he aligns on the inside receiver to the wide side of the field at a 7-yard depth (Diagram 5-32).

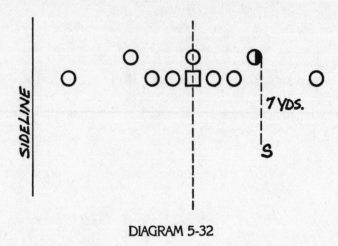

DIAGRAM 5-32

Keys and Reactions

When Corner, Stay, or Invert coverage is used, the primary key for the safety is the quarterback. His reactions are based on the movements of the quarterback. When man-to-man coverage is used, the 45-degree alignment allows the safety to look at his man as the primary key and to the quarterback as his secondary key. When Free Safety is used, his keys and reactions are determined by the job he is to perform in this coverage.

The first reaction of the safety is determined by the coverage that is used. When man-to-man coverage is used, he uses the same three-step shuffle as the defensive halfback. When Corner, Stay, or Invert coverage is used, he takes four quick steps in place on the snap of the ball. This gives him the time needed to read and react properly to his key. When Free Safety is called, his first reaction is determined by the responsibility he is given.

When man-to-man coverage is employed, the safety reacts to his keys in the same manner as the defensive halfback. The reactions of the safety to the movements of the quarterback are determined by the zone coverage that is being used.

When the quarterback uses a passing action that goes wider than the offensive guard, he reacts in the following manner:

1. *Corner.* He sprints in the same direction as the quarterback to the deep, outside one-third zone (Diagram 5-33).

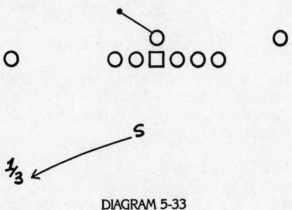

DIAGRAM 5-33

2. *Stay.* He drops in the middle one-third zone (Diagram 5-34).

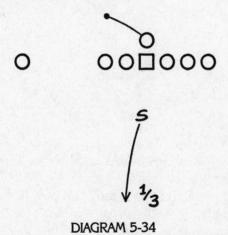

DIAGRAM 5-34

3. *Invert.* He sprints in the same direction as the quarterback to the flat zone and levels at 7 yards (Diagram 5-35).

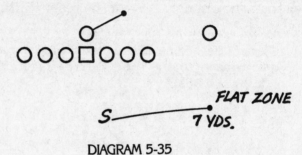

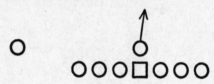

DIAGRAM 5-35

When the quarterback uses a passing action between the outside legs of the offensive guards, he reacts by dropping in the middle one-third zone on Corner, Stay, and Invert coverages (Diagram 5-36).

DIAGRAM 5-36

When the quarterback either gives or runs the ball, and the safety is sure the threat of pass is gone, he reacts "Up" to make the tackle (Diagram 5-37).

When Free Safety is used, the reactions of the safety are not directly governed by the actions of the quarterback. He reacts to various keys as follows:

1. *Blitz.* He reacts to the snap of the football and fires through a predetermined area.
2. *Prevent.* He reacts to the snap of the ball and plays as a centerfielder in baseball.
3. *Lock On.* He reacts to his receiver and plays him man-to-man.
4. *Normal.* He stays at his 12-yard alignment and attacks the ball. He is free to go where the ball goes.

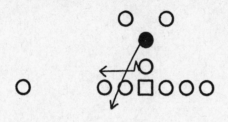

DIAGRAM 5-37

Run Responsibilities

When a quick-hitting play is run from tackle to tackle, such as a dive or quick trap, the safety is the last line of defense if the ballcarrier passes the defensive linemen and linebackers. He attacks the runner with controlled speed, while being very careful to make a sure tackle. He is not expected to make the play at the line of scrimmage, but to prevent the long gain (Diagram 5-38).

When a slow-hitting play is run from tackle to tackle, or when any other play is run outside the tackles, the safety attacks the play from the inside-out. On this type of play he can be more aggressive because he has the defensive halfback, away from the play, rotating behind him. The defensive halfback is in the position of preventing the long gain (Diagram 5-39).

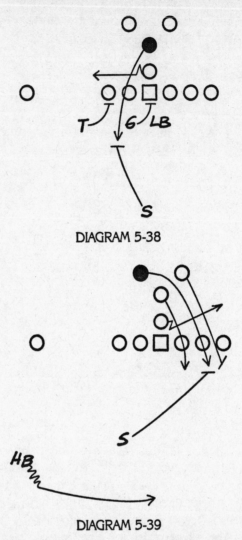

DIAGRAM 5-38

DIAGRAM 5-39

Versus the option, the safety first checks his zone. When he is sure the threat of pass is gone, he executes his normal run responsibilities. His responsibilities vary when Invert or man-to-man coverage is used.

When Invert is called, he sprints toward the flat zone to the side of the play and is usually responsible for the quarterback. There are situations, depending on the Defensive Game Plan, when he could be responsible for the pitchman (Diagram 5-40).

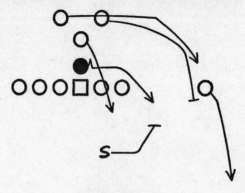

DIAGRAM 5-40

When man-to-man coverage is employed, he stays with his man until the ball crosses the line of scrimmage and then attacks the ballcarrier (Diagram 5-41).

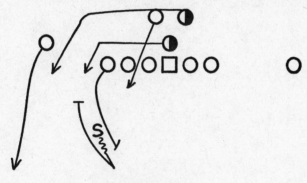

DIAGRAM 5-41

Pass Responsibilities

The pass responsibilities of the safety are very similar to those of the defensive halfback. His methods and techniques for defending against the completed pass in both man-to-man and zone coverages are the same.

When man-to-man coverage is employed, unlike the defensive halfback who covers the first receiver to his side of the field, the safety's responsibilities vary with the offensive formation being used.

COMBINATION-60
TEAM DEFENSES

6

Before we get into a detailed analysis of the *Team Defenses*, it is essential to answer the following five questions:

1. What is a *Team Defense?*
2. What is a *Combination Defense?*
3. How do they affect the various defensive units?
4. What is the purpose of a Team Defense?
5. What is the purpose of a Combination Defense?

A *Team Defense* tells the defensive line that they are to execute the same technique in the same direction. An example of a Team Defense is "Slant-Right." This tells the entire defensive line that they are to "Slant" to the right (Diagram 6-1).

A *Combination Defense* tells the defensive line that they are to execute various techniques in the same direction. An example of a Combination Defense is "Slant-Tackles Up-Right." This tells the defensive guards that

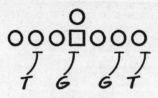

DIAGRAM 6-1

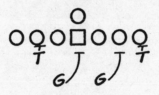

DIAGRAM 6-2

they are to "Slant" to the right and the defensive tackles are to execute an "Up" to the right (Diagram 6-2).

The use of either a Team or Combination defense has little effect on the secondary. Their responsibilities are determined by the coverage that is employed and are not affected by the defense used by the front. An exception to this rule is Gap and Tough, which is explained in Chapter Seven.

The linebackers and the ends are concerned only with the direction of the defense and not the techniques used by the linemen. The linebackers and the ends use the same techniques when both "Slant" and "Up" are used. The only defensive unit that uses both the technique call and the direction call is the defensive line.

One purpose of the Combination-60 Defense is to cause confusion for the opponents. Both Team and Combination defenses fulfill this purpose. This confusion affects the individual blocker as well as the coach and quarterback who are attempting to fashion a successful attack.

By looking at "Slant-Right," "Slant-Left," "Up-Right," and "Up-Left," the problems faced by the opponent become apparent (Diagrams 6-3, 6-4, 6-5, 6-6).

By analyzing the recognition and blocking problems

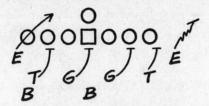

DIAGRAM 6-3 "Slant-Right"

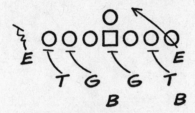

DIAGRAM 6-4 "Slant-Left"

DIAGRAM 6-5 "Up-Right"

DIAGRAM 6-6 "Up-Left"

of the left offensive tackle, the problems of all the blockers become evident. As an effective blocker, he must recognize the defenders in his immediate blocking area. The three main defenders are: the right defensive guard, the right defensive tackle, and the first linebacker to his side of the center.

When "Slant-Right" and "Slant-Left" are employed, he sees the same basic alignment as far as the defensive

guard, defensive tackle, and middle linebacker are concerned. Yet, he is attacked by two different defenders
coming from different sides. On "Slant-Right," he is attacked by the right defensive guard, coming from the
offensive tackle's right. When "Slant-Left" is used, he is
attacked by the right defensive tackle, coming from the
offensive tackle's left. On "Up-Right," the defensive guard
is aligned on him, while the defensive tackle is aligned on
the outside of the tight end. When "Up-Left" is used, the
defensive tackle is aligned on him while the defensive
guard is aligned on the center. The only position that
remains constant in all four defenses is that of the middle
linebacker.

If you look at the four defenses from the viewpoint
of the coach and quarterback, you will see a different
alignment for each defense. When "Slant-Right" and
"Slant-Left" are used, the defensive front appears to be
unbalanced because of the alignment of the offside linebacker (Diagram 6-7). When the defensive linemen execute
their techniques, the defense is nearly balanced. There is
no advantage to attacking one side of the defensive front
as opposed to the other, even though it does appear weaker
to the onside in the basic alignment (Diagram 6-8).

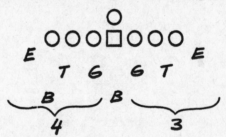

DIAGRAM 6-7 "Slant-Right"

When compared to the "Slant" alignment, the "Up"
alignment gives the appearance of an entirely different
defense. This may indicate to the offense that they use a
different type of attack other than the one used against the
"Slant." In reality, the "Up" is nothing more than the

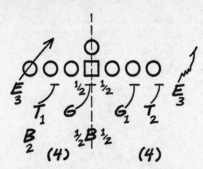

DIAGRAM 6-8 "Slant-Right"

"Slant" with the defensive linemen closer to their points of attack.

The most confusing point, as far as an opponent is concerned, is that the offense never can plan to see a particular defense at any time. There are eight Team Defenses, a nearly unlimited number of Combination Defenses, and Gap and Tough.

Even though confusion for the offensive team is a basic reason for using the various Team and Combination defenses, there are certain instances when a particular Team or Combination should be used. These instances result from a definite offensive tendency acquired from the extensive scouting report, or from situations that arise during a game.

When an offensive team, in some particular situation, shows a tendency to run a particular play, this indicates the use of a Team Defense. The following are two examples of such a situation:

1. An offensive team on first down and ten, when the ball is on the right hash mark, has run an outside play to their left 25 out of 34 times. (This information was acquired from a two-game scouting report). This type of statistic indicates the use of "Slant-Right." If the offensive team follows its tendency, the defensive linemen are not only in a good position to stop the play but are attacking at the correct angle for excellent pursuit. If the ball is run

to some other area or the ball is thrown, the team is still in a good position to protect against any offensive play. This is a benefit of a balanced defense (Diagram 6-9).

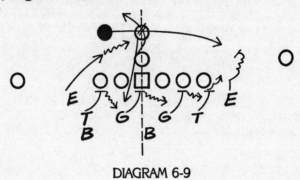

DIAGRAM 6-9

2. An offensive team on third down and ten, no matter where the ball is on the field, has used a sprintout pass to their right 16 out of 20 times. (This information was acquired from a two-game scouting report). This type of statistic indicates the use of "Up-Left." If the offensive team follows its tendency, the "Up" will allow excellent pressure on the quarterback and a quick outside rush will be gotten by the left defensive tackle and the left defensive end. If the team uses another run or pass, the defense is still in excellent position (Diagram 6-10).

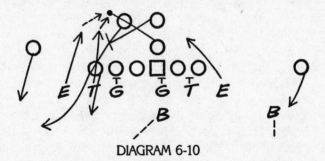

DIAGRAM 6-10

The situations that require the use of a particular Combination Defense are discussed in Chapter Seven.

DEFENSIVE CALLS

The design of the defensive huddle is an integral part in the communication of the defensive call. The left linebacker and the safety align with their backs to the offensive team, 1 yard in front of the ball. This distance allows them to step back to the ball to look to the sideline for a defensive signal without stepping across the line of scrimmage. The defensive line aligns 2 yards deeper than the signal callers. They are shoulder to shoulder, facing the line of scrimmage. They stand with their hands on their knees and their heads up, looking at the signal callers. The defensive ends align perpendicular to the line of scrimmage facing each other. They are 2 yards from the line of scrimmage and aligned off the outside shoulder of the defensive tackles. They stand up straight with their arms at their sides, looking at the signal callers. The defensive halfbacks and right linebacker stand erect behind and between the defensive line. They have their arms at their sides and they are looking at the left linebacker and safety. The right linebacker stands in the middle and is flanked by both halfbacks (Diagram 6-11).

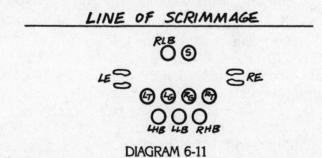

DIAGRAM 6-11

The signals are flashed into the signal callers. They step back to their 1-yard depth, face the huddle, and make the calls. The linebacker calls the Team or Combination defense first, then the safety makes the secondary call.

When a Team Defense is being used, the linebacker could call "Slant" or "Up" followed by the direction, when the direction is given from the sideline. Many times,

however, the direction is not given and it is up to the
linebacker to make the direction call when the offensive
team comes over the ball. His direction call is determined
by a tendency that is acquired from the scouting report.
When this situation occurs, the linebacker calls the technique in the huddle followed by "listen for the call." This
tells the defensive front that they must listen for the
direction when the offensive team comes over the ball.

After the linebacker makes his call, the safety makes
the secondary call. Since the direction of the secondary
flow is determined by the actions of the quarterback when
a zone coverage is used, no direction call is made in the
huddle. When "Corner" or "Invert" is called, the safety
follows this with "listen for the call." This alerts the offside
linebacker, onside end, and halfbacks that a change may
be made in the call prior to the snap of the ball. This
change occurs when the safety feels that the secondary
coverage called in the huddle could be ineffective against a
particular offensive formation.

When the offensive team comes over the ball, both the
left linebacker and the safety make a call. When "listen for
the call" is said by the linebacker in the huddle, he calls the
direction of the defense. He uses the words *right, left, in,*
and *out.* This is called a "live" call. When the direction is
given in the huddle, the linebacker still makes a "dead"
call. This call has no effect on the defense but is made to
prevent the offense from keying on the direction call.

The safety makes two calls. The first call is made
when the offense comes over the ball. When either "Corner" or "Invert" is called in the huddle, the safety may
make a change in the coverage or keep the original call.
When he wants the original coverage to remain in effect,
he calls "Play." When he wishes to alter the coverage, he
makes the following calls:

1. *"Stay."* This is called only when "Corner" is called in
   the huddle. The coverage changes from "Corner" to
   "Stay."

2. *"Invert Red."* (Right)—This changes the coverage to "Invert" to the defensive right, when offensive action goes that way. When offensive action goes to the left or the quarterback employs dropback pass action, "Stay" coverage is automatic.

3. *"Invert Lou."* (Left)—Same as "Invert Red," except to the left.

When "Corner" or "Invert" is called in the huddle, these preliminary calls are "live." When any other secondary is called in the huddle, the safety still makes a "dead" call. Like the linebacker's "dead" call, it has no effect on the defense and is done only to confuse the offense.

The safety makes the second call after he reads the action of the quarterback. When zone coverage is used, this call determines the direction of flow for the secondary. He calls "Run" or "Pass" preceded by right, left, or drop. He also makes the "Run" or "Pass" call when man-to-man coverage is used; but right, left, or drop are "dead" calls in this coverage.

FRONT DEFENSES

The following is a description of the various Team Defenses. The individual assignment of each member of the defensive front is given.

"Slants"

"Right"

Left linebacker and end—offside
Right linebacker and end—onside
Defensive line—"Slant" to the right
(Diagram 6-12)

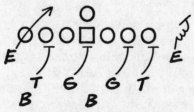

DIAGRAM 6-12 "Slant-Right"

"Left"

Left linebacker and end—onside
Right linebacker and end—offside
Defensive line—"Slant" to the left

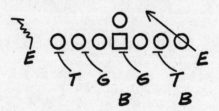

DIAGRAM 6-13 "Slant-Left"

"In"

Left linebacker and end—offside
Right linebacker and end—offside
Left tackle and guard—"Slant" to the right
Right tackle and guard—"Slant" to the left
(Diagram 6-14)

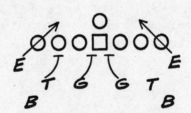

DIAGRAM 6-14 "Slant-In"

Since this Team Defense has no onside line-backer, there is no defender to cover the hook area. This is a definite weakness of this particular defense. To compensate for this weakness, man-to-man coverage is often used with this defense.

If both guards were to use their basic "Slant" technique, they could collide while executing this defense. To eliminate this problem, the guards are told to "Slant" to a point between the midline and near shoulder of the center. Their responsibility also changes when "In" is used. They no longer are responsible for both sides of the center, but only the G gap to their side (Diagram 6-15).

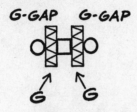

DIAGRAM 6-15

"Out"

Left linebacker—"Blitz" the left G gap
Right linebacker—"Blitz" the right G gap
Both ends—onside
Left tackle and guard—"Slant" to the left
Right tackle and guard—"Slant" to the right
(Diagram 6-16)

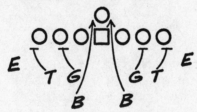

DIAGRAM 6-16 "Slant-Out"

Like the "Slant-In," this defense has no defender to cover the hook area. Man-to-man coverage is also frequently used with this defense. Unlike "Slant-In," this defense provides a strong inside rush.

"Ups"

"Right"

Linebackers and ends—same as "Slant"
Defensive line—"Up" to the right
(Diagram 6-17)

DIAGRAM 6-17 "Up-Right"

"Left"

Linebacker and ends—same as "Slant"
Defensive line—"Up" to the left
(Diagram 6-18)

DIAGRAM 6-18 "Up-Left"

"In"

Linebacker and ends—same as "Slant"
Left tackle and guard—"Up" to the right
Right tackle and guard—"Up" to the left
(Diagram 6-19)

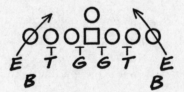

DIAGRAM 6-19 "Up-In"

Like "Slant-In," an adjustment is necessary for
the guards. They align on the same target point that
they use while executing the "Slant-In," and they are

responsible for the G gaps to their side. Man-to-man pass coverage is also frequently used with this defense.
(Diagram 6-20)

DIAGRAM 6-20

"Out"

Linebackers and ends—same as "Slant"
Left tackle and guard—"Up" to the left
Right tackle and guard—"Up" to the right
(Diagram 6-21)

Like "Slant-In," man-to-man coverage is frequently used with this defense.

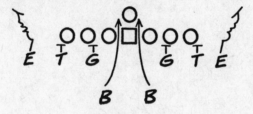

DIAGRAM 6-21

SECONDARY

The goal of the Combination-60 secondary is to be as uncomplicated as possible to teach and learn, yet complicated and flexible enough to cause reading problems for opposing coaches, quarterbacks, and receivers. This is accomplished with two-deep, three-deep, and four-deep coverages, and two different man-to-man coverages. The two-deep coverages are *Corner* and *Invert*. These are the only secondary coverages that can be changed after the defensive huddle and before the snap of the ball. The three-deep coverages are *Stay, Free Safety Blitz,* and *Free Safety Lock-on.* The four-deep coverages are *Free Safety* and *Free Safety Prevent.* The two man-to-man coverages are regular man-to-man and a special man-to-man that is played with Gap and Tough.

Corner

This is a two-deep coverage that, depending on the passing action of the quarterback, can become a three-deep coverage (Diagram 6-22).

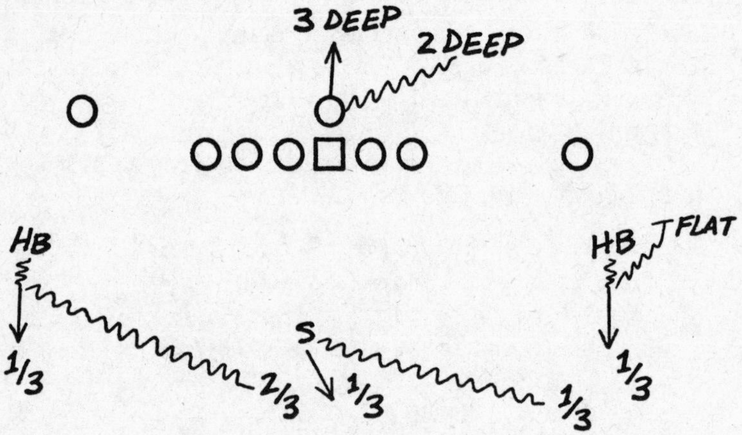

DIAGRAM 6-22

Corner is a two-deep zone when the quarterback uses a passing action that goes wider than the offensive guards. It is a three-deep zone when the quarterback uses a dropback passing action. When this situation occurs, Corner becomes Stay.

Versus the run, Corner is a two-deep zone with the halfback rotating up to the side of the action as the outside contain. The safety checks the deep outside one-third zone to the side of the action. After the threat of a pass has gone, he attacks the play from the inside-out. The halfback away from the offensive action flows through the secondary toward the play. Since the entire defense is balanced, this places an extra defender to the side where the ball is run (Diagram 6-23).

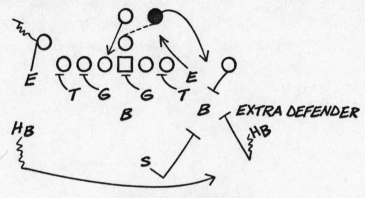

DIAGRAM 6-23 "Slant-Left"

The basic alignment of the safety indicates that he could have a problem covering a wide receiver who is running a deep pattern in the outside one-third zone. The safety is aided in this situation by the defensive front and the halfback who covers the flat zone. Whenever a quarterback uses a passing that goes wider than either offensive guard, he is attacked by two defenders from the outside. This outside rush forces the quarterback to pull up and to release the ball quickly. The quick release prohibits the receiver from running a deep pattern and reduces the distance the safety has to cover to be in proper position to defend against a completion (Diagram 6-24).

The halfback, who is responsible for flat-zone coverage, also aids the safety with his coverage. As the halfback levels in the flat zone, he collides with the wide receiver when he attempts to run past the defensive halfback. This slight delay of the receiver gives the safety additional time to get to the deep outside one-third zone.

The double outside pass rush is not only a reason for the use of Corner coverage, but it was also a primary reason for the development of the Combination-60. We were facing many opponents who were using passing actions that were wider than the offensive guards (sprint-

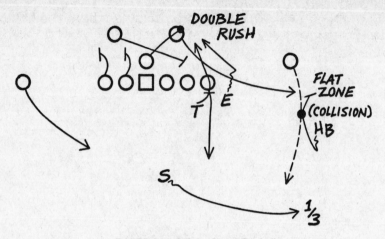

DIAGRAM 6-24 "Slant-Right"

out, rollout, and play action), and we wanted to disrupt the action and force the quarterback to throw sooner than he desired. We also wanted flat-zone coverage to the side of the offensive action. The Combination-60 provides a double pass rush versus a wide passing action, and gets quick flat-zone coverage from the halfback to the side of the action. When passing action is to the onside of the defense, the quarterback is attacked by the onside tackle and the onside end. When passing action is to the offside of the defense, he is attacked by the offside end and the offside linebacker (Diagram 6-25).

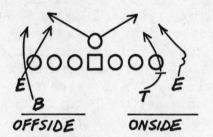

DIAGRAM 6-25 "Slant-Right"

Invert

This is also a two-deep coverage that, depending on

the passing action of the quarterback, can become a three-deep coverage (Diagram 6-26).

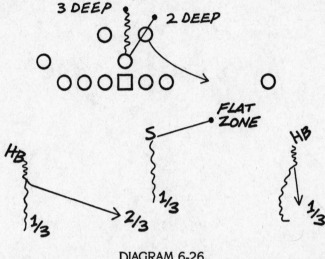

DIAGRAM 6-26

Invert, like Corner, is a two-deep zone when the quarterback uses a passing action outside the guards, and a three-deep zone when he uses a passing action between the offensive guards. When he uses a passing action between the guards, Invert becomes Stay.

Versus the run, Invert also is a two-deep zone. The safety quickly reacts to the side of action and attacks it from the inside-out. The halfback, to the side of action, checks the deep outside one-third zone, then reacts up as the outside contain. The halfback away from action plays the same way as Corner. Like Corner, this puts an extra defender to the side the ball is run. Unlike Corner, the extra defender attacks from the inside-out (Diagram 6-27).

One purpose of Invert coverage is to prevent the safety from getting beat in the deep outside one-third zone against a receiver who has an exceptionally wide split. Even though the double rush helps the safety when Corner coverage is used, there is a point where the wide receiver is too wide for the safety to cover, if he runs a deep outside pattern and the quarterback uses a passing action to that side. Invert coverage allows the halfback, to the side of the wide passing action, to cover the deep outside one-third zone, while getting flat-zone coverage by the safety.

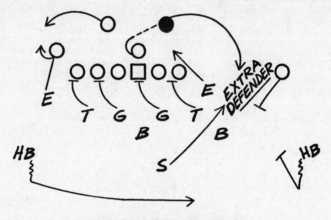

DIAGRAM 6-27 "Slant-Left"

Invert coverage is often used against an offense that employs a wide receiver who has a very wide split, and who runs the option to that receiver. If Corner coverage is used, the halfback would be too far out in his initial alignment to cover the pitchman effectively. Invert coverage allows the offside linebacker or the onside end (whoever is to the side of the option) to cover the pitchman, while the safety takes the quarterback (Diagram 6-28).

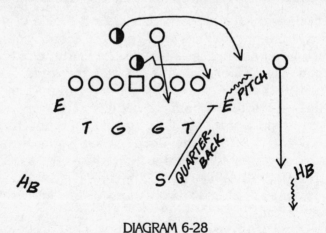

DIAGRAM 6-28

The safety has the option of changing the secondary coverage prior to the snap of the ball, when "Corner" or "Invert" is called in the huddle. There are two reasons the safety can make the change. He may change the secondary when he feels that, because of the offensive formation, he cannot properly execute the coverage that was called. When the scouting report shows a team has a tendency to use a particular play or plays from a formation, the safety is instructed to execute the change against that formation. The change can be made when the offensive team aligns in the formation or when they use motion to get into it. The change can be made any time prior to the snap of the ball.

There are several reasons why the safety feels he cannot execute the called coverage. The following are some of those reasons, along with the changes, when "Corner" is called in the huddle:

1. When the offensive team employs a pro-formation, and the wide receivers are split too wide for the safety to cover them in the deep outside one-third zone, and it is a passing situation, he calls "Stay." This gives the halfbacks the deep outside zones and eliminates the difficult coverage for the safety (Diagram 6-29).

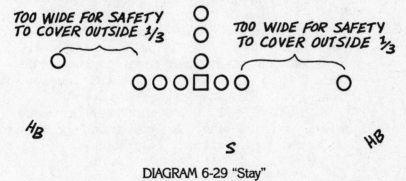

DIAGRAM 6-29 "Stay"

2. When the offensive team employs the same formation as #1, but it is a running situation, the safety calls "Invert" to the wide side of the field or strength of the formation. This is determined by the scouting report. This change allows the safety to fill quickly

when the ball is run to the side of the call, while still eliminating his pass coverage problems to both sides. Even though the safety aligns at a 7-yard depth (Invert alignment), he is still in good position to play the deep middle zone if the quarterback drops back or uses a passing action to the side away from the Invert (Diagram 6-30).

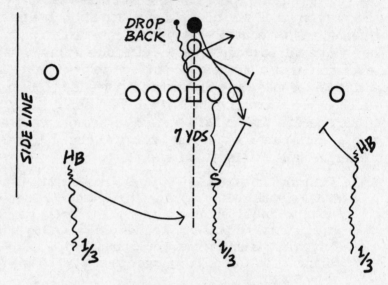

DIAGRAM 6-30 "Invert-Red"

3. When the offensive team employs a single wide receiver, who is split too wide for the safety to cover in the deep outside one-third zone, the safety calls "Invert" to that side. When the quarterback uses a passing action to that side, the halfback covers the deep outside zone and this eliminates the problem coverage for the safety. As in situation #2, the safety uses his Invert depth (Diagram 6-31).

When "Invert" is called in the huddle, it is very rare for the call not to be changed prior to the snap of the ball. Since the safety often aligns over an offensive guard, it is very difficult for him to cover the flat zone or to play the option to the side opposite his alignment (Diagram 6-32).

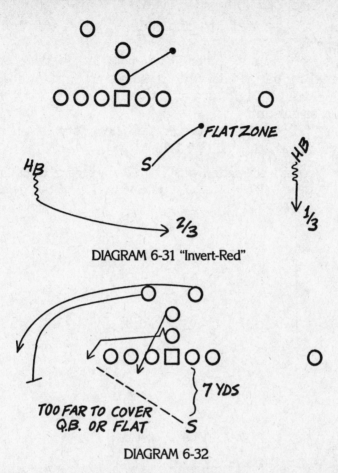

DIAGRAM 6-31 "Invert-Red"

DIAGRAM 6-32

For this reason, the safety changes the call to the side of his basic alignment. This puts him in a good position to cover the flat zone and the option to the side of the call. When the quarterback uses dropback passing action or a wide passing action away from the change call, or when a running play is employed to that side, Stay coverage adequately protects against both the run and the pass.

At one time, we attempted to change the alignment of the safety when "Invert" was called. Rather than aligning over a guard, he aligned over the center. In this alignment, he was too far removed from both sides to cover the flat zone or option to either side. This is one reason we decided to call the "Invert" to the side of the safety's basic alignment.

The only time "Invert," when called in the huddle, remains unchanged is when a scouting report indicates that it would be safe and effective to use the coverage in certain situations.

The following are the changes the safety makes when "Invert" is called in the huddle:

1. Versus a formation with no wide receivers, he calls "Invert" (Red or Lou) to the wide side of the field (Diagram 6-33).

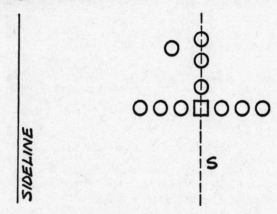

DIAGRAM 6-33 "Invert-Red"

2. Versus a formation with one wide receiver, he calls "Invert" to the wide receiver side (Diagram 6-34).

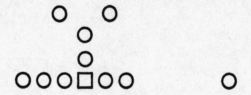

DIAGRAM 6-34 "Invert-Red"

3. Versus a formation with a wide receiver to both sides, "Invert" is called to the wide side of the field (Diagram 6-35).

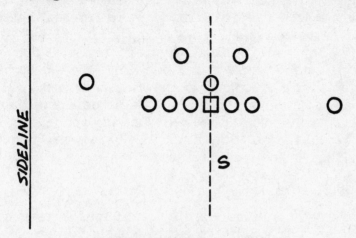

DIAGRAM 6-35 "Invert-Red"

Stay

This is a three-deep coverage against all passing actions (Diagram 6-36).

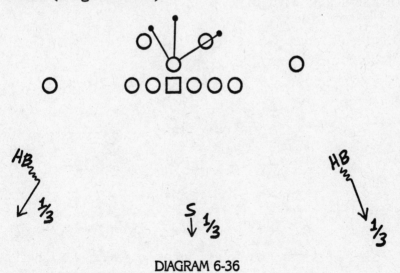

DIAGRAM 6-36

This defense is often called in passing situations and is used automatically when the safety calls "Stay" prior to the snap, after "Corner" is called in the huddle. It is also automatic when the quarterback uses a dropback passing action or a passing action away from an "Invert Red" or an "Invert Lou" call. Unlike Corner and Invert, it does not provide a double rush to the side where the quarterback uses a passing action outside the offensive guard. For this reason, it is called more often in the defensive huddle against teams that use dropback passing action.

Versus the run, Stay automatically becomes Corner to the side of the action (Diagram 6-23).

Free Safety (Blitz, Lock-On, Normal, Prevent)

Even though there are four different coverages involved with Free Safety, the coverages are different only for the safety. The basic coverage is the same for the other defenders.

It is a three-deep coverage that is easily converted to a four-deep by various placements of the safety. Unlike Stay, the deep middle one-third zone is covered by either an end or a linebacker (Diagram 6-37).

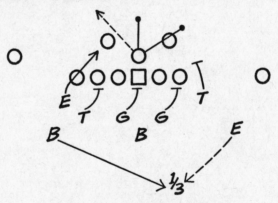

DIAGRAM 6-37 "Slant-Right"

This coverage has one particular weakness. The flat zone away from a wide passing action is not covered. Also, the flat zone to the side of the offside linebacker is also

uncovered on dropback passing action. This weakness is
taken into consideration prior to using the coverage. It is
not employed against an offense that has a tendency to
throw the ball into the flat zone away from quarterback
passing action or into the flat zone on dropback action.

Free Safety is never used with "Slant-In or Out" or
"Up-In or Out." There is one main reason for this rule. On
dropback passing action, the offside linebacker's pass
coverage responsibility is the deep middle one-third zone.
He is usually a better athlete than the defensive end and we
prefer to have him cover that zone on dropback passing
action. If "In" is employed, there would be no flat-zone
coverage or two linebackers in the middle one-third zone,
since both linebackers would be offside (Diagram 6-38).
When "Out" is used, there would be double flat-zone
coverage and no defenders in the deep middle one-third
zone (Diagram 6-39).

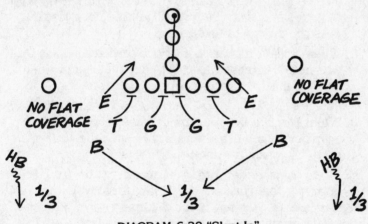

DIAGRAM 6-38 "Slant-In"

Free Safety is similar to "Stay" in two ways. It is used
more often in passing situations than running situations
and there is no double rush against the quarterback who
uses a wide passing action. Unlike Stay, it is a very flexible
coverage. With the four safety variations, many different
goals can be achieved. The following are some of those
goals:

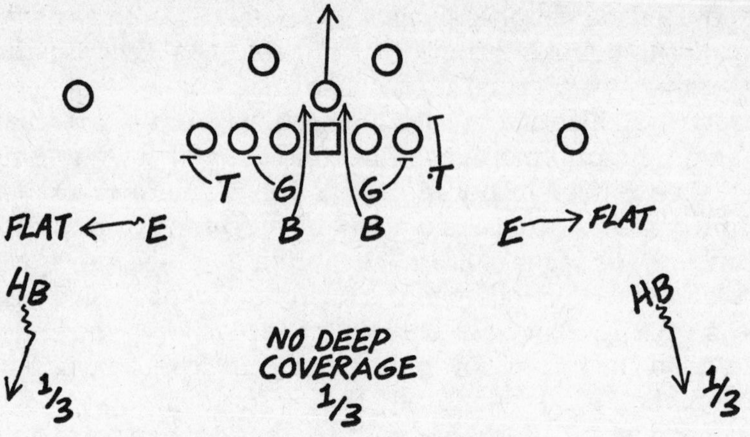

DIAGRAM 6-39 "Slant-Out"

1. When we wish to surprise the quarterback with an unexpected pass rusher, *Blitz* can be used. This is also very effective against the run when the safety attacks the ballcarrier in the backfield for a loss and puts the offense off-schedule.

2. When a team has an exceptional receiver, *Lock-On* can help neutralize him. This provides additional man-to-man coverage while still playing zone coverage.

3. When *Normal* is used, the defense becomes a four-deep coverage with the safety having the ability to go to the pass or attack the ballcarrier.

4. When it is a definite passing situation and the offensive team needs a large gain for a first down or touchdown, *Prevent* is the defense to use. With the safety playing as a deep centerfielder, the possibility of a long completion is greatly decreased. This is accomplished while still playing a normal three-deep coverage under the safety. The safety is also in a good position to protect against the long run.

Versus the run, Free Safety is similar to Corner, except the halfback to the side of the run must be sure the threat of pass is gone in his deep outside one-third zone before he levels to 4 yards. Unlike Corner, he does not have the safety to protect the outside one-third zone behind him. Because of the original placement of the defender who replaces the safety, he cannot get to the deep outside one-third zone as quickly as the safety. This causes the halfback to react a bit slower when run action is to his side (Diagram 6-40).

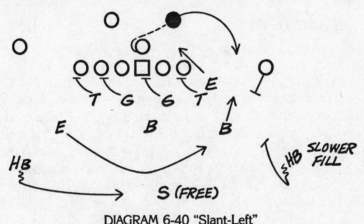

DIAGRAM 6-40 "Slant-Left"

Man-to-Man (regular)

This coverage is similar to Stay in that it does not provide a double pass rush when the quarterback uses a wide passing action to the wide receiver side, while sending a back out of the backfield to that side. Either the offside linebacker or the onside end, depending on the direction of the front call, must pick the back up and cannot rush the passer (Diagram 6-41). For this reason, we do not like to employ this coverage against an opponent who uses a wide passing action while sending receivers out of the backfield to the passing action side.

Man-to-Man is also less effective against a team that runs the option to the wide receiver side of the formation. Zone coverages have the capability of double-covering either the quarterback or the pitchman against an option

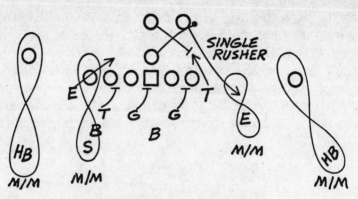

DIAGRAM 6-41 "Slant-Right"

offense. This coverage does not have that capability, since the defensive halfback, to the side of the option, must stay with his receiver until the ball crosses the line of scrimmage. Therefore, depending on the direction of the front call, either the onside end or the offside linebacker is solely responsible for the pitchman, and the onside tackle or the offside end is responsible for the quarterback (Diagram 6-42).

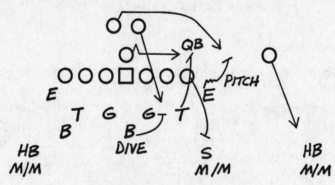

DIAGRAM 6-42 "Slant-Right"

COMBINATION DEFENSES

7

The main purpose of a Combination Defense, like a Team Defense, is to confuse the opponent. Combination Defenses confuse the individual blockers, but are mainly employed to confuse the coach and the quarterback who are attempting to solve the defense. This confusion is accomplished by the defensive alignment. Even though the same target points are attacked when a Team and Combination Defense are used, they are attacked from different alignments. By looking at "Slant-Right," a Team Defense; and "Slant-Guards Up-Right," a Combination Defense; this point is made clear (Diagrams 7-1, 7-2).

Opponents view these as two different defenses and attempt to attack them in different ways. In reality, both defenses attack the same areas and could be attacked by the offense in a similar fashion.

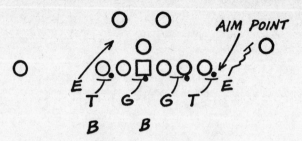

DIAGRAM 7-1 "Slant-Right"

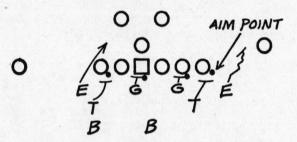

DIAGRAM 7-2 "Slant-Guards Up-Right"

Like Team Defenses, there are certain instances when a particular Combination Defense should be employed. These instances are a result of a definite offensive tendency that was acquired from the scouting report, or from situations that arose during a game.

The following are examples of circumstances that indicate a certain Combination Defense should be used:

1. An offensive team, on third down and more than 5 yards, has used a sprint-out pass to the tight-end side of the formation 10 out of 25 times. They ran a dive play to the split-end side of the formation also 10 out of 25 times. (This information was acquired from a two-game scouting report.) This type of statistic indicates the use of "Slant-Tackles Up-to the Tight-End Side." This allows the defensive tackle, to the tight-end side, to play on the tight end and delay his release. It also gives that tackle the opportunity to put on a good outside pass rush. The

tackle to the split-end side is in a good position to defend against the dive by being close to the line of scrimmage and by causing blocking problems, by his initial alignment, for the offensive guard and tackle. Like the entire Combination-60 package, if the team does not follow its tendency, the defensive team is still in a good position to stop any play (Diagram 7-3).

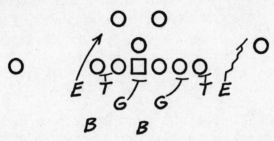

DIAGRAM 7-3 "Slant-Tackles Up-to the Tight End"

2. During a game, it is determined that the left offensive tackle is a poor blocker and cannot effectively block either the right defensive guard or tackle. To take advantage of this weakness, the right defensive tackle or guard, depending on the direction of the call, can play "Up." This puts them in an excellent position to defeat the block of the left offensive tackle. Examples of two possible Combination calls are as follows: "Slant-Right Tackle Up-Left," or "Slant-Right Guard Up-Right" (Diagrams 7-4, 7-5).

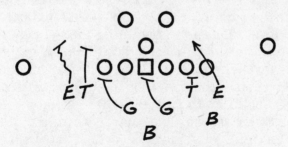

DIAGRAM 7-4 "Slant-Right Tackle Up-Left"

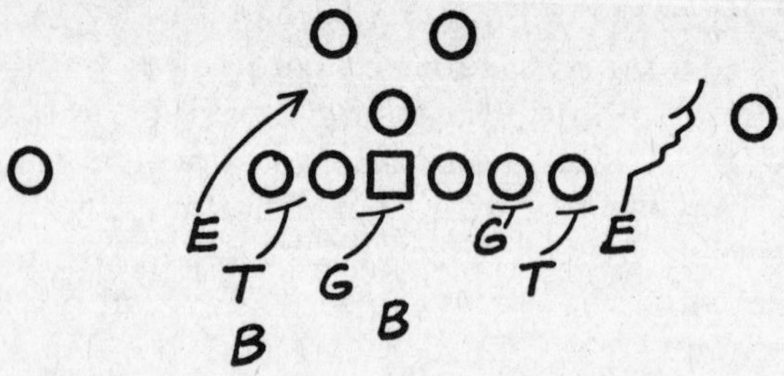

DIAGRAM 7-5 "Slant-Right Guard Up-Right"

DEFENSIVE CALLS

There is no significant difference in the procedure used for calling a Combination Defense or a Team Defense. The only minor difference is that a Combination defensive call has more words than a Team defensive call. This sometimes presents a time problem for the signal caller, as well as a problem for the coach, who attempts to signal the defense to the left linebacker (signal caller). This problem is partially eliminated when a Combination Defense is part of the defensive game plan that is prepared from scouting reports, when it is determined that "Slant-Left Tackle Up-Right" will be used during a particular game. This defense is practiced during the week with a code name that is much shorter and simpler to communicate. Rather than saying "Slant-Left Tackle Up-Right," the defense is called "Slant-Right 1." This alerts the left defensive tackle and tells him that he must play "Up" when he hears "1" after "Slant-Right." This is known as a *game special*. When a Combination Defense is created during a game, the full call is made. When it becomes a problem for the coach to signal the defense to the linebacker, he uses a messenger to run the call into the huddle. Often a defensive guard is used for this purpose. The guard goes directly to the left linebacker and tells him the call. The linebacker then assumes his normal signal calling responsibility.

VARIOUS COMBINATIONS

The number of Combination Defenses is limited only by the imagination of the coach. One possible weakness of the Combination-60 defensive package is that the coach could fall into the trap of using Combination Defenses without a definite purpose except to create defensive variety. For Combination Defenses to be effective, they should be devised with a specific purpose in mind. Even though confusion for the opponent is a basic reason for the use of Combination Defenses, there must be a definite reason for using a particular defense.

When the coach designs a Combination Defense with the purpose of stopping a particular phase of an offense, he must be aware of the fact that the defense could be weaker against another phase of that offense. For example, "Slant-Right Tackle Up-Right" is a good defensive call against a team that uses a sprint-out type of pass to the defensive right and likes to hit the tight end to that side. This gives the defensive right a good angle to prevent the tight end from an outside release, while being in a good position to put on an effective outside pass rush (Diagram 7-6). However, if the team also runs a lead off-tackle play to the same side, both the offensive tackle and tight end have good angles to block the defensive tackle and guard (Diagram 7-7). A better defensive call might be "Slant-

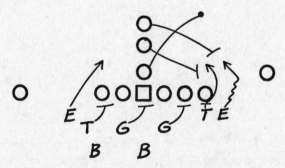

DIAGRAM 7-6 "Slant-Right Tackle Up-Right"

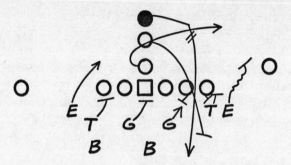

DIAGRAM 7-7 "Slant-Right Tackle Up-Right"

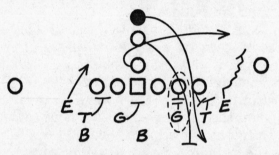

DIAGRAM 7-8 "Slant-Right Side Up-Right"

Right Side Up-Right." This takes away the good blocking angle of the offensive tackle and still serves the initial purpose of the defense (Diagram 7-8).

GAME SPECIALS

Game specials are Combination Defenses that are devised as part of the defensive game plan. They are established as a result of information that is acquired from the scouting report of the upcoming opponent. The following are some of the reasons game specials are devised:

1. To take advantage of a weak offensive lineman.
2. To stop a running play that the opponent has shown a tendency to use in a particular down and distance situation.

3. To put quick outside pressure on a quarterback who uses a wide passing action and has shown a tendency to falter under a severe pass rush.

4. To put strong pressure on a dropback quarterback in a passing situation while still covering a middle screen or draw. This is often accomplished by playing an "Up" and by having the offside defensive guard "Slant." Since he is responsible for the middle screen and draw, the use of "Slant" slows his pass rush enough to be in a good position to read and to stop either of these plays (Diagram 7-9).

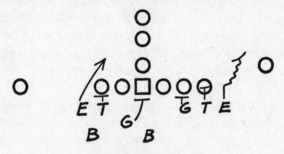

DIAGRAM 7-9

As explained earlier in this chapter, game specials are given a code name for ease of communication and are practiced by the defensive team all week. It is rare to use more than three game specials a week. However, the total number of Combination Defenses is often more than three. This is determined by the amount of adjustments that are required during a game. There are games when numerous Combination Defenses are used and games when only Team Defenses, Gap, and Tough are employed.

GOAL-LINE AND SHORT-YARDAGE DEFENSES

Gap and Tough are the only defenses in the Combination-60 package when the defenders use some different techniques from those used when Team and Combination Defenses are employed. In both Gap and Tough, the linebackers and secondary use the same techniques, while the defensive linemen and ends use different techniques for each.

These two defenses are considered the gambling phase of the Combination-60 package. There are several reasons for this. There is severe pressure placed on the secondary by their basic alignment and techniques. Gap and Tough are employed in many situations other than goal-line and short-yardage situations. For example, while playing an undefeated opponent who had one of the finest passing games in the state, we used Gap and Tough 60 percent of the time. We held the opponent scoreless until two minutes remained in the game. We won 14 to 7, while sacking the quarterback 12 times for 126 yards in losses. We also intercepted two passes and returned one for 54 yards.

Gap or Tough is not always employed in special goal-line and short-yardage defenses; Team or Combination Defenses are also often used. This prevents an opponent from expecting a particular defense in a certain situation and the element of surprise remains.

Gap

This is a penetrating defense. It is very effective against an offense that has slowly developing plays. It gives the defensive linemen an opportunity to disrupt the play before it totally develops. Gap is also effective against an offense that is expected to pass. It puts a strong pass rush on very quickly.

Halfback

The defensive halfback plays man-to-man coverage, but his alignments, techniques, and the offensive personnel he covers are different from regular man-to-man coverage. His coverage responsibilities are as follows:

1. When the halfback has only a tight end (any end who is split less than 2 yards from the offensive tackle) to his side, he is responsible for the first

back out of the backfield to his side of the formation
(Diagrams 7-10, 7-12).

2. Versus any other formation, except the one described in #1, he is responsible for the first receiver
to his side of the formation. This is the same as his
regular man-to-man coverage responsibility. (Diagrams 7-11, 7-12).

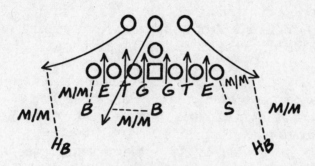

DIAGRAM 7-10

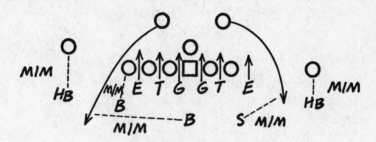

DIAGRAM 7-11

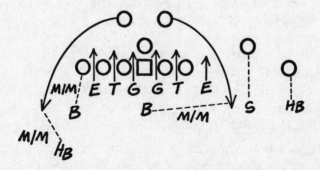

DIAGRAM 7-12

When his coverage responsibility is a wide receiver, he aligns 1 yard off the line of scrimmage with his nose on the outside ear of the receiver. Rather than aligning at a 45-degree angle, he aligns with his shoulders parallel to the line of scrimmage with his outside foot slightly back. On the snap of the ball, he "bumps" the receiver and then plays man-to-man coverage. This tight defensive alignment puts a great deal of pressure on the halfback; but the rush, put on by the defensive front, forces the quarterback to throw early. This helps the halfback with his coverage (Diagram 7-11).

Versus a tight end, he uses his normal zone alignment and stance, but his depth is 4 yards rather than 7. When a back comes out of the backfield on a pass route, he plays him man-to-man (Diagrams 7-10, 7-12).

If no back comes out to his side during a passing play, the halfback plays as a Free Safety and goes to the ball. His responsibilities versus the run are the same as when regular man-to-man coverage is employed.

Safety

He also plays man-to-man coverage, and like the defensive halfbacks, his alignments, techniques, and the personnel he covers are different from regular man-to-man coverage. His coverage responsibilities are as follows:

1. Versus a two-tight end (tight slot) formation, he is responsible for the tight end (tight slot) to the defensive right (Diagram 7-10).

2. Versus a formation with a tight end and a split end, he is responsible for the first back out of the backfield to the split-end side (Diagram 7-11).

3. Versus a formation with a tight end to one side and twin receivers to the opposite side, he is responsible for the inside twin receiver (Diagram 7-12).

When playing against a tight end (tight slot), he aligns with his nose on the outside shoulder of the tight end (tight slot), 1 yard off the ball (Diagram 7-10).

Versus a split end, he aligns with his nose on the midline of the defensive end to the split-end side of the formation. His depth is determined by the down and distance. He may be as deep as 3 yards off the ball or as tight as 1 yard. From this alignment, he can cover a back out of the backfield to his side as well as the pitchman on the option. He is also in a good position to help to the other side of the formation on both passing and running plays (Diagram 7-11).

Versus a twin receiver set, he aligns on the inside receiver and uses the same techniques as the defensive halfbacks (Diagram 7-12). On all running plays to his side, the safety has outside contain responsibility and must force everything to the inside.

Left Linebacker

He plays over the center and uses the same techniques he employs when he is the onside linebacker in both Team and Combination Defenses. He also has the same responsibilities versus the running game. Versus a pass, he is responsible for the first back out of the backfield to the two-receiver side of the formation. When no back comes out to that side, he plays his normal zone coverage (Diagram 7-11).

Right Linebacker

He also plays man-to-man coverage, and like the safety and halfback, his alignment, techniques, and the personnel he covers are different from regular man-to-man coverage. His coverage responsibilities are as follows:

1. Versus a two-tight end (tight slot) formation, he is responsible for the tight end (tight slot) to the defensive left (Diagram 7-10).
2. Versus a formation with a single tight end, he is responsible for that man (Diagrams 7-11, 7-12).

He uses the same alignment and techniques as the safety and is also responsible for outside contain to his side of the formation.

End

The end aligns in the E gap as tight to the line of scrimmage as possible. When there is no tight end (tight slot) he aligns as though one is in the normal position. He uses the same three-point stance that is employed by the defensive linemen. On the snap of the ball, he shoots the gap and attacks the play. He is careful not to overpenetrate and take himself out of the play. On the option, he is responsible for the quarterback (Diagrams 7-11, 7-12).

Tackle

He aligns in the T gap as tight to the line of scrimmage as possible, and executes the same charge as the defensive end (Diagrams 7-10, 7-11, 7-12).

Guard

He aligns in the G gap as tight to the line of scrimmage as possible, and executes the same charge as the defensive tackle (Diagrams 7-10, 7-11, 7-12).

The following diagrams show the various alignments against different offensive sets:

1. A two-tight end offense (Diagram 7-10)
2. A normal pro-set offense (Diagram 7-11)
3. A wide-twin offense (Diagram 7-12)

Tough

This, unlike Gap, is not a penetrating defense. The purpose of Tough is to control the line of scrimmage and to prevent the center or either of the offensive guards from getting to the middle linebacker (left linebacker). This is not the best defense to use against a team that is expected to pass. It does not provide as quick a pass rush as Gap. Since there is little line penetration, this defense provides excellent pursuit.

Halfbacks, Safety, and Linebackers

These positions play the same way for Tough as they do for Gap.

End

Versus a tight end (tight slot), the end aligns in a two-point stance, with his nose on the inside shoulder of the tight end as tight to the line of scrimmage as possible. His shoulders are square to the line of scrimmage with his inside foot slightly back. On the snap of the ball, he steps with his outside foot and hits the tight end with a hand shiver. He then reacts to the inside and looks for the off-tackle play or the quarterback on the option. For the Tough to be effective, the defensive end can never be blocked inside by the tight end. Versus a split end, he plays the same as Gap (Diagrams 7-13, 7-15).

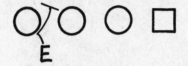

DIAGRAM 7-13

Tackle

He uses an "Up-In" alignment. On the snap of the ball, he steps to the near hip of the offensive guard and prevents him from getting to the middle linebacker (left linebacker). He uses a charge that is very similar to his basic "Slant" technique. The one difference is that the first step is a bit more parallel than the basic "Slant" (Diagrams 7-14, 7-15).

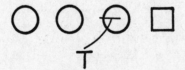

DIAGRAM 7-14

Guard

He uses the same alignment he employs when the Gap is used. On the snap of the ball, he steps into the near hip

of the center and prevents him from getting to the middle linebacker (left linebacker). Diagram 7-15 shows the Tough versus a pro-set formation.

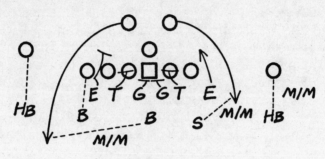

DIAGRAM 7-15

THE COMBINATION-60 DEFENSE IN ACTION

8

This chapter includes four offensive plays, and two Team Defenses and one Combination Defense that have been used to stop each of these offensive plays. The individual techniques and responsibilities of those defenders at or near the point of offensive attack are also covered. Since the Combination-60 package holds so many possibilities, it would be impossible to cover all the ways to stop particular offensive plays. For this reason, this chapter is limited to certain defenses; however, these are by no means the only ways to defend the offensive plays that are described.

There are also numerous ways to run the particular offensive plays that are used in this chapter. For the purpose of simplicity, only one method of running each play is described.

OFF-TACKLE PLAY

"Slant-Right"—"Corner" (Diagram 8-1)

This defense not only provides fine coverage at the point of attack, but it also provides excellent pursuit, since

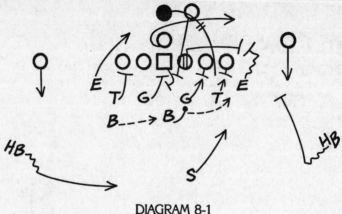

DIAGRAM 8-1

the line is "Slanting" in the same direction in which the offensive play is being run.

The right defensive end reads the pull of the offensive guard and closes to the inside in an attempt to squeeze the play. He is also aware that the quarterback could keep the ball after the fake, so he does not close down to the point where he loses outside leverage on the ball.

The right defensive tackle "Slants" into the tight end, who attempts to block him. He meets the blocker on his second step and fights through the block to eliminate the possibility of a hole developing between himself and the defensive end. Since his charge technique ("Slant") is taking him in the direction of the play, the least he should accomplish is a stalemate with the tight end.

The right defensive guard "Slants" to the tackle, who attempts to block him. He fights through the block in the same manner as the defensive tackle. He must also fight to get at least a stalemate with the offensive tackle.

When the head of the center goes down the line to the onside, the onside linebacker reads it as a cutoff block and steps in the same direction as the center. This move puts him in a good position to defeat the block of the center and move to the ballcarrier. He is also aware of the running back who is filling for the pulling offensive guard. When he is attacked by this offensive player, he keeps outside leverage, which puts him in a good position to stop the play.

The halfback, to the side of the play, reads it as a run and levels at 4 yards. He keeps outside leverage on the ball. When the ballcarrier crosses the line of scrimmage, he attacks him from the outside-in.

The safety reads the run and reacts to the ballcarrier from the inside-out, as the defensive halfback flows through the secondary as the last line of defense against the run.

"Slant-Left"—"Invert Red" (Diagram 8-2)

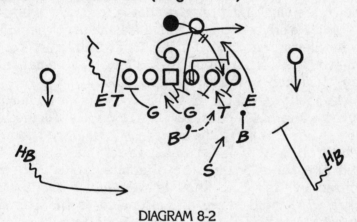

DIAGRAM 8-2

Unlike "Slant-Right," this defense does not provide quick pursuit by the defensive linemen, since they are "Slanting" in a different direction than the offensive play is being run. Yet, this defense provides a more explosive defensive attack, since the defensive end is crashing through the point where the offensive play is designed to go. This defense also aligns the offside linebacker near the point of offensive attack. When he reads his key properly, he is in a position to shut down the play.

The right defensive end executes a *Pinch* on the tight end. This forces the tight end inside and seriously hinders his effectiveness as a blocker on the defensive tackle or the onside linebacker. After executing the Pinch technique, the defensive end is in a good position to meet the play at the point of the quarterback-running back mesh. If the pulling offensive guard quickly reads the attack of the defensive end, he may attempt to block him. This puts the guard too deep in the offensive backfield and causes too much congestion for the play to be effective. It also stops any blocker from handling the offside linebacker and frees him to handle the running back.

The right defensive tackle "Slants" to the offensive tackle. When he reads both the tight end and the offensive tackle stepping in the same direction as his "Slant," he executes his normal "Slant" but is prepared to fight through the blocking pressure that will be exerted by the tight end. He strives to establish a stalemate so that a hole does not develop in the defensive front. His attack on the offensive tackle eliminates that offensive lineman as a possible blocker on the onside linebacker.

The right defensive guard "Slants" to the center and eliminates him as a possible blocker on the onside linebacker. After attacking the center, he is in a good position to attack the play. This is because the offensive guard has pulled and the block of the offensive tackle has been hindered by the "Slanting" left defensive tackle. The blocker who could cause him problems is the offensive back who is filling for the pulling offensive guard. However, this blocker most often attempts to cut off the onside linebacker.

The onside linebacker reads and reacts in the same manner for both "Slant-Right" and "Slant-Left."

The offside linebacker reads the block of the tight end. As the blocker steps to the inside, the linebacker steps up and in the same direction as the blocker. This puts him in the off-tackle hole. At this point, he is looking for a pulling guard or a lead back. If the offensive pulling guard attempts to block the defensive end, there is no blocker to take him and he should stop the play. If the pulling guard attempts to block him, he forces the guard inside and does not allow a hole to develop.

The defensive halfback, to the side the play is run, first checks his deep outside one-third of the field. When he reads run and is sure the threat of pass is gone, he levels at 4 yards and plays the same as Corner coverage.

The safety aligns at his Invert depth, over the offensive guard to the side of the widest receiver. Unlike Corner, he does not have to be concerned about the deep outside one-third of the field. This, along with his 7-yard depth, allows him to react more quickly to the run. As he reads run, he attacks the play from the inside-out. Like the halfback, he is sure all threats of a pass are gone before he commits himself to the run.

"Slant-Right Side Up-Left"—"Man-to-Man" (Diagram 8-3)

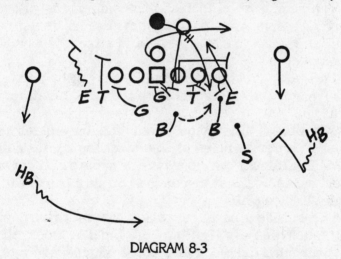

DIAGRAM 8-3

This defense, like "Slant-Left," provides the explosive defensive attack by the end, while still permitting good pursuit by the right defensive guard and tackle, since they are using an "Up" technique. Since the right defensive guard and tackle are not slanting in the opposite direction in which the play is being run, they are in a better position to defeat the blocks of their opponents and to get more quickly to the ballcarrier. Man-to-man coverage also provides quicker fill by the safety, since the block of the tight end brings him directly to the point of attack.

The right defensive end uses the same techniques and reacts in the same manner in this defense as he did when "Slant-Left" was employed.

The right defensive tackle steps into the offensive tackle and fights through the pressure of his block. He also eliminates the possibility of the tackle blocking the onside linebacker.

The right defensive guard steps to the center. Since he is on the play side of the center, he should have no trouble beating his block and getting quickly into the play. Like "Slant-Left," he must be aware of the back who is filling for the pulling offensive guard.

The defensive halfback to the side of the play stays with his receiver until the ball crosses the line of scrimmage. He then levels at 4 yards and attacks the ball from the outside-in.

The safety reads the action of the tight end. As he blocks down, the safety reacts to the run and attacks the ballcarrier.

The onside linebacker reads the movement of the offensive center as he steps to cut off the right defensive guard. The linebacker moves in the same direction as the center and is again aware of the running back who may attempt to block him.

The offside linebacker reads the movement of the tight end. When the tight end attempts to block him, he fights through the block and keeps outside leverage. The Pinch technique, executed by the right defensive end, aids the linebacker in his play against the tight end.

OPTION PLAY

One of the purposes of the Combination-60 Defense is to cause reading problems for the quarterback when he attempts to run the option. This is accomplished by giving the quarterback different looks at the point where he must make the decision to keep or pitch the ball.

"Up-Right"—"Stay" (Diagram 8-4)

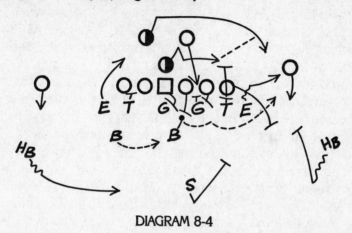

DIAGRAM 8-4

The right defensive end executes his normal three-step shuffle across the line of scrimmage. When he sees that no blockers are coming from the inside to attack him, he holds and reads the play. When he reads option, he knows his responsibility is the pitchman. He keeps outside leverage on the pitchman and stays with him until the whistle blows. Even if the quarterback keeps the ball beyond the line of scrimmage, the defensive end stays with the pitchman in case of a late downfield pitch.

The right defensive tackle executes his "Up" technique on the tight end. His attack prohibits the tight end from running an effective arc block on either the right defensive end or the defensive halfback to the side of the play. After executing his "Up" technique, the tackle holds his ground and plays the quarterback in a "soft" manner. He does not attack the quarterback until he turns up inside or comes to the target point. If the quarterback pitches prematurely (prior to reaching the target point), the tackle attacks the pitchman from the inside-out.

The right defensive guard attacks the offensive tackle and fights the pressure of his block. He cannot allow himself to be blocked inside, for this would create a hole between himself and the defensive tackle and give the quarterback an area in which to run. He is also aware of the dive back and attacks him unless he is sure he does not have the ball.

The onside linebacker reads the movement of the center and steps to the same side that the center steps. He is also aware of the left offensive guard, as he is not being attacked by a defensive lineman and is free to attempt to block him. Since the movement of the center has the linebacker stepping in the direction of the offensive guard, he should be in a good position to defeat his block. Even though he is responsible for the ball when the option is run, he first checks the dive back and then flows to the quarterback and finally the pitchman.

Since Stay coverage is being used, the defensive half-back must be sure the threat of pass is gone in his outside deep one-third zone before he can react to run. When he is sure the threat of a pass is gone, he reacts up and attacks the ball from the outside-in. He now plays the pitchman along with the onside defensive end.

The safety must be sure the threat of a pass is gone in his deep middle one-third zone. When he is sure the threat of a pass is gone, he reacts up and attacks the ball from the inside-out.

"Slant-Left"—"Free Safety Normal" (Diagram 8-5)

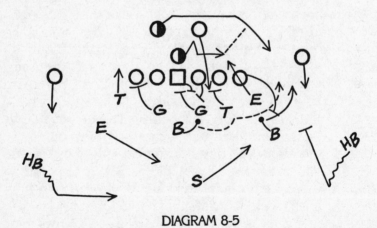

DIAGRAM 8-5

On initial alignment, this defense gives a completely different look at the corner than "Up-Left"—"Stay." There is a defender in the E gap (right defensive tackle) and a defender on the outside shoulder of the tight end (right defensive end). Since Free Safety is being used, the offside linebacker is in a Walkaway or Switch alignment. This gives the appearance of a four-deep zone coverage with a safety inverted to the flanker side of the offensive formation.

The right defensive end executes a Pinch technique on the tight end; this hinders him from using an effective arc block on the offside linebacker. After executing his Pinch, the defensive end attempts to attack the quarterback on the quarterback-dive-back mesh point. This quick attack on the quarterback normally forces him to pitch the football prematurely. The end attacks the quarterback with fury. This rough attack makes the quarterback very aware of the end the next time he attempts to run the option and could cause an offensive error.

The right defensive tackle "Slants" to the offensive tackle and eliminates him as a possible blocker on the onside linebacker. Upon reaching his target point, he is in a good position to check the dive back. He attacks the dive back unless he is completely sure that he does not have the ball. When he is sure the dive back is not the ballcarrier, he gets into his proper pursuit angle and attacks the ball.

The right defensive guard "Slants" to the center. He keeps outside leverage on the center and like the right defensive tackle, checks the dive back before flowing to the outside.

The onside linebacker reads the movement of the center and steps in the same direction as the center. He checks the dive back, then continues to flow to the outside. His play is the same as on "Up-Right."

The offside linebacker is responsible for the pitchman. From his Walkaway alignment, he takes his initial step to the defensive onside. When he recognizes the option, he keeps outside leverage on the pitchman and stays with him until the whistle blows. He is also aware of the tight end's arc block, and fights *through* the block, not around it.

The defensive halfback, to the side of the option, plays in the same manner he uses when Stay is called.

The safety is free and from his depth he has the ability to read the option and to determine who has the ball. Once he determines the ballcarrier, he attacks the ball.

Tough—Man-to-Man (Diagram 8-6)

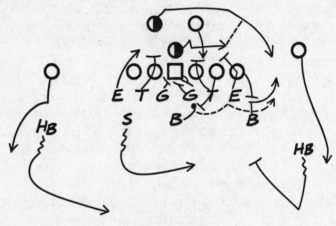

DIAGRAM 8-6

The right linebacker (linebacker to the tight end) aligns on the outside shoulder of the tight end and "bumps" him as he attempts to release. As the tight end attempts to force the linebacker inside, he keeps outside leverage and is solely responsible for the pitchman.

The right defensive end steps into the tight end from his inside alignment. This helps eliminate the possibility of the tight end blocking the defensive end inside. It also knocks the tight end off-stride and makes an arc block on the linebacker more difficult. After making contact with the tight end, the defensive end reacts inside and attacks the quarterback.

The right defensive tackle "Slants" to the hip of the offensive guard and keeps him off the middle linebacker.

After contact with the offensive guard, the tackle reacts to the dive back. There is a good possibility that the defensive tackle could meet the quarterback at the quarterback-dive-back mesh point. This could disrupt the play before it has a chance to fully develop.

The right defensive guard steps into the near hip of the center and prevents him from blocking the middle linebacker. After contact is made he reacts to the play and gets into pursuit.

The middle linebacker (left linebacker) reacts to the initial action of the quarterback and steps to the same side that the center steps. He immediately looks to the dive back, since the dive back is his first responsibility. He is aware of the left offensive tackle, since he is the only lineman to the play side who is not attacked by a defender and could block him. When the linebacker is sure that the dive back does not have the ball, he continues to the outside and checks the quarterback, then the pitchman.

The defensive halfback to the side of the play uses his man-to-man techniques; he does not react to run until the ball crosses the line of scrimmage. When the wide receiver attempts to block the halfback, he fights through the block and forces the ballcarrier inside. He fights to keep the blocker away from his legs.

The safety reacts to the play, but he makes sure there is no throwback possibility to any backfield player on his side before he pursues the play. He attacks the play from the inside-out and discourages any cutback by the ballcarrier.

A fine feature of the Combination-60 Defense is the capability of double-covering any facet of the option when Corner, Invert, or Free Safety Normal is used. When a team has a particular phase of the option that is extremely good, the defensive coach may want to put an extra man on that phase. The following are just a few examples:

1. *"Slant-Right"*— *"Corner" (double the quarterback).*
   In this defense the right defensive tackle is responsible for the quarterback along with the defensive

end. This puts single coverage on the pitchman by the defensive halfback (Diagram 8-7).

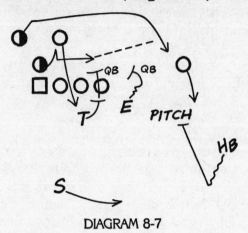

DIAGRAM 8-7

2. *"Slant-Left"— "Corner" (double the pitchman).* The right defensive end executes his Pinch technique and is responsible for the quarterback. The offside linebacker and the right defensive halfback are responsible for the pitchman. This puts single coverage on the quarterback, with help from the onside linebacker coming from the inside (Diagram 8-8).

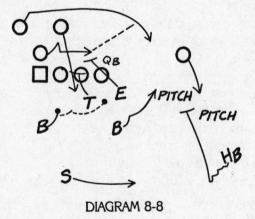

DIAGRAM 8-8

3. *"Up-Left" — "Free Safety Normal" (safety double quarterback).* The safety aligns as a middle mon-

ster over the center and 7 yards deep. When he reads the side to which the option is being run, he attacks the quarterback from the inside-out. The right defensive end executes his Pinch technique and also attacks the quarterback. The offside linebacker, from his Walkaway alignment, takes the pitchman and gets slow help from the right defensive halfbacker coming from the outside-in (Diagram 8-9).

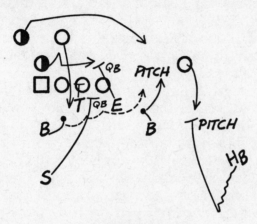

DIAGRAM 8-9

TRAP PLAY

"Slant-Right"—"Corner" (Diagram 8-10)

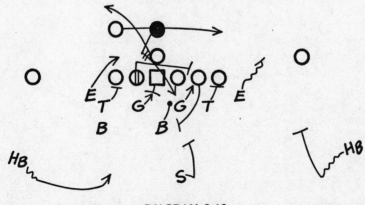

DIAGRAM 8-10

As the left defensive guard "Slants" to the center, he realizes the center is moving toward him. The defensive guard keeps his shoulders parallel to the line of scrimmage and goes through the center. He does not allow the center to cut him off and thus create a large hole between himself and the other defensive guard.

The onside linebacker reads the movement of the center and reacts to his step toward the left defensive guard by stepping straight ahead and filling to the tail of the center. He is aware of the left offensive guard who is attempting to block him. As he feels the pressure of the offensive guard, he fights through the pressure and steps up to make the play.

As the right defensive guard "Slants" to the tackle, he is aware that neither the man on whom he was originally aligned (offensive guard), nor the man to whom he is "Slanting" (offensive tackle), is attempting to block him. After making contact with the offensive tackle, he quickly closes inside and looks for the trapping offensive guard. He meets him in the hole and forces a stalemate, thus eliminating an effective trap.

"Up-Left"—"Invert" (Diagram 8-11)

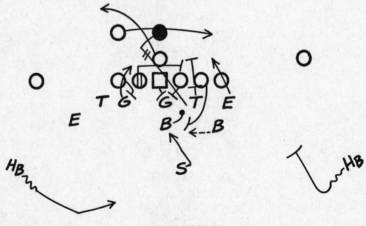

DIAGRAM 8-11

The left defensive guard executes his "Up" technique on the tackle and is sure to keep from getting hooked. He fights through the head of the tackle and slides to the inside so that he is in excellent position to stop the play.

The onside linebacker reads the movement of the center as he attempts to block the right defensive guard. He steps in that direction and is aware of the offensive tackle who is coming toward him. He steps up in an attempt to meet the running back in the hole and to miss the block of the offensive tackle. If the tackle makes contact with the linebacker, he fights through the pressure of the blocker and forces the running back to go wider than he originally planned.

The right defensive guard attacks the center and feels the double-team. He drops to his right knee and turns his shoulders perpendicular to the line of scrimmage while shooting his hands between the two blockers. He fights to split the double-team and creates a pile at the point of the offensive attack.

The right defensive tackle attacks the offensive tackle and feels his release to the outside. He looks to the inside and reacts to the trapping guard by keeping his shoulders parallel to the line of scrimmage and stepping into him. He fights through the trapper and forces a stalemate at the hole.

"Slant-Left Side Up-Right"—"Corner" (Diagram 8-12)

The left defensive guard aligns on the center and plays the double-team in the same manner as the right defensive guard plays it in "Up-Left."

The onside linebacker reacts to the movement of the center. He steps to the defensive right and steps up to beat the block of the left offensive tackle. Since the tackle is being attacked by the right defensive guard, the linebacker may find that he is not being blocked by any offensive player.

The right defensive guard "Slants" into the left offensive tackle and prevents him from blocking the onside linebacker. After executing his "Slant" technique, the defensive guard reacts to the inside and locates the ballcarrier.

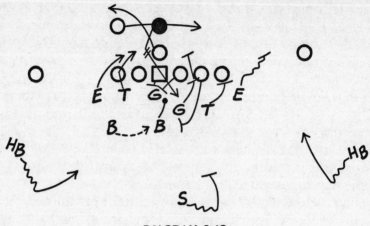

DIAGRAM 8-12

SPRINT PASS

Defending the sprint pass was one of the basic reasons for the development of the Combination-60 Defense.
We wanted to put strong outside pressure on the quarterback, while still covering the flat zone to the side of the
play and the deep outside one-third zone to that side. Any
time Corner or Invert coverage is used, all three of these
goals are achieved.

"Up-Right"—"Corner" (Diagram 8-13)

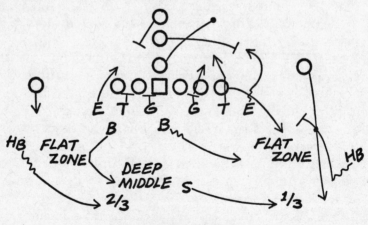

DIAGRAM 8-13

The right defensive end takes his three-step shuffle across the line of scrimmage. When he reads sprint pass, he attacks the quarterback. He fights through the blocking back and never goes around him. He is very careful to keep the blocker away from his legs.

The right defensive tackle attacks the tight end and prohibits him from an easy pass release. After using his "Up" technique on the tight end, he attacks the quarterback. He, like the defensive end, goes through any blocker who attempts to take him.

The right defensive guard executes his "Up" technique on the tackle and attacks the quarterback from the inside-out.

The onside linebacker reads the pass block of the center and follows his zone coverage rules.

The defensive halfback reacts to the pass and levels at 7 yards (the flat zone). As he levels, the defensive halfback attacks the wide receiver in an attempt to slow him from getting to the deep outside one-third zone. He covers the deepest receiver in his zone and goes to the ball when it is thrown.

The safety reads the pass and reacts to the deep outside one-third zone. He covers the deepest receiver in his zone and goes to the ball when it is thrown.

"Slant-Left"—"Invert" (Diagram 8-15)

"Slant" does not provide as quick a pass rush as "Up." Yet, when the defensive line makes the proper read, an effective pass rush does result.

The right defensive end executes his Pinch technique through the tight end. This prohibits the tight end from running a quick pass pattern. The defensive end then attacks the quarterback. When he reads pass, he alters his angle into the backfield in an attempt to cut the quarterback off and to not allow the quarterback to get outside of him (Diagram 8-14).

The right defensive tackle "Slants" to the tackle and reads the pass. He fights through the block of the tackle and attacks the quarterback from the inside-out.

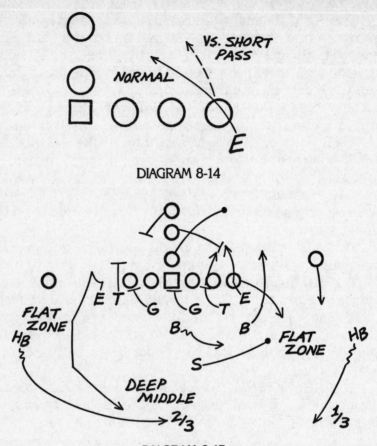

DIAGRAM 8-14

DIAGRAM 8-15

The onside linebacker reads the pass and follows his zone rules.

The offside linebacker reads the sprint pass and attacks the quarterback from the outside-in. He, like the defensive end, goes through any blocker who attempts to block him.

The defensive halfback to the side of the play reacts to the deep outside one-third zone. He makes sure he is as deep as the deepest offensive player in his zone. He reacts to the ball once it is thrown.

The safety reads the pass and sprints to the flat zone. As in all zone coverages, he covers the deepest receiver in his zone and reacts to the ball when it is thrown.

"Slant-Tackles Up-Right"—"Free Safety Normal" (Diagram 8-16)

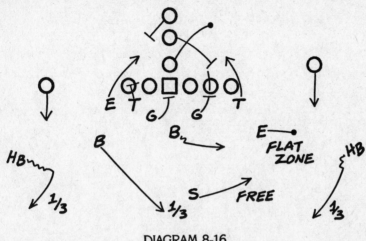

DIAGRAM 8-16

The right defensive end aligns in a Walkaway and covers the flat zone when he reads sprint pass action to his side. Unlike Corner and Invert, this coverage does not provide a double rush against the quarterback, since the defensive end has a pass coverage responsibility.

The right defensive tackle and the onside linebacker play the same as "Up-Right."

The right defensive guard "Slants" to the offensive tackle. As he reads pass, he goes through the tackle and attacks the quarterback from the inside-out.

The offside linebacker, from his Walkaway alignment, reads sprint pass and reacts to the deep middle one-third zone. The halfback to the side of the play reads pass and reacts to the deep outside one-third zone. The safety is free and reacts to the action of the quarterback and the ball when thrown (Diagram 8-16).

THE COMBINATION-60 SCOUTING SYSTEM AND DEFENSIVE GAME PLAN

9

ORGANIZATION OF THE SCOUTING SYSTEM

The scouting program is one of the most important aspects of the Combination-60 package. The information acquired from the scouting report determines the Team and Combination Defenses that will make up the Defensive Game Plan.

Scouting consists of viewing the team one week before we face them, as well as analyzing a film of the opponent in action. While coaching in high school, we were very fortunate to have a film exchange in our league. Our scouts exchanged our latest game film with our opponent immediately after viewing their game. In this way, we had a report on the opponent's latest game and a film of the game they played prior to the one we saw in person, and our opponent had the same thing on us. We use the same system at Widener University.

The week before our game, three scouts view the opponent's game. Each scout is given particular responsibilities during the game. They are as follows:

175

1. *Scout #1.* He uses the *Backfield Defensive Scouting Booklet,* which contains 25 scouting forms (Diagram 9-1). These 25 pages include enough blanks for 100 offensive plays. He records the action of the backfield on every offensive play. This includes the quarterback; the set backs; and the flanker, slot, or wing. During the game, this is the only facet of the offense with which he is concerned.

2. *Scout #2.* He uses the *Line Defensive Scouting Booklet.* This contains the same forms as the backfield booklet and also contains 25 forms. He records the action of the offensive line on every offensive play. This also includes the split end. He also has the responsibility of recording the down and the distance that the opponent must go for a first down, the opponent's position on the field, the yard line the ball is on at the beginning of the play, and the gain or loss on each play. The scout circles "R" when the ball is on or approximately 1 yard to the open field side of the right hash mark. He circles "L" when the ball is on or approximately 1 yard to the open field side of the left hash mark. On all other ball placements he circles "M," for the middle of the field. When recording the yard line, the scout puts a + (plus sign) before the yard line when the team being scouted is in the opponent's half of the field. When the team being scouted is in its own half of the field, a − (minus sign) is put before the yard line.

3. *Scout #3.* He helps scout #2 get all the vital information (yard line, position on the field, down and distance, and gain or loss) prior to the snap of the ball. He pays particular attention to the offensive personnel of the opponent and looks for weaknesses and strengths. He also notes the defense the opponent is facing to determine how they attack particular defenses. If either scout #1 or scout #2 needs help, he aids him.

During halftime, scout #1 records in his book all the information from the book of scout #2. This is a very

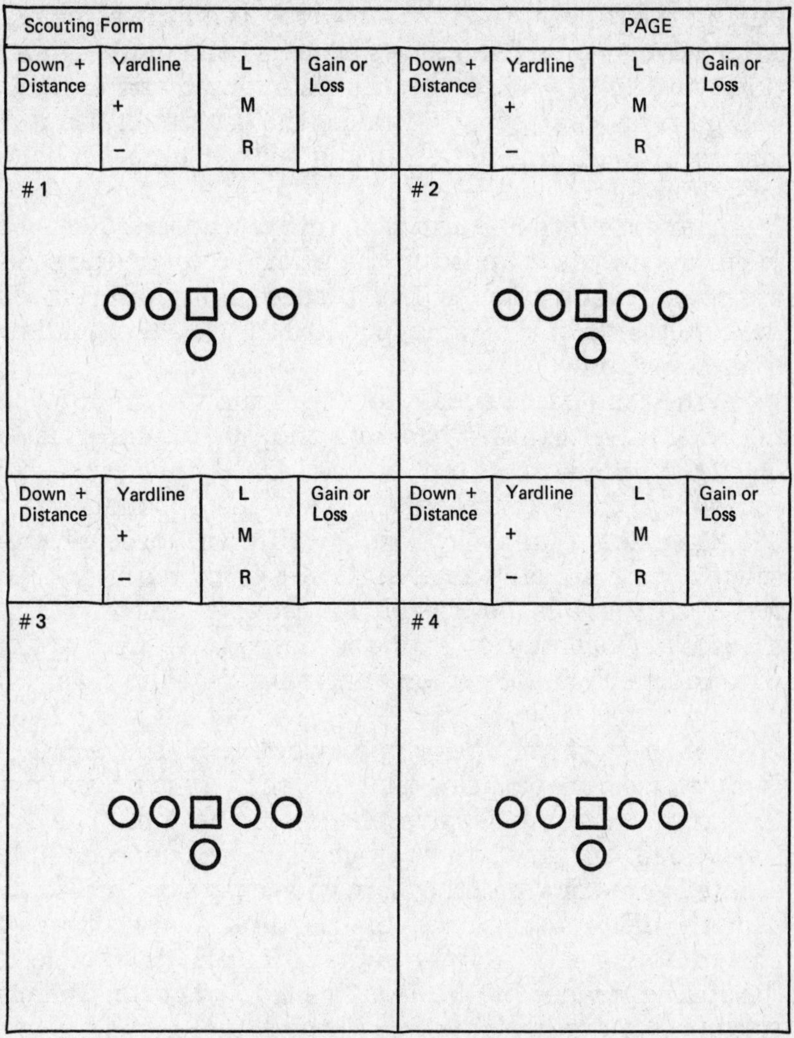

Scouting Form						PAGE	
Down + Distance	Yardline + –	L M R	Gain or Loss	Down + Distance	Yardline + –	L M R	Gain or Loss

1

◯ ◯ ☐ ◯ ◯
◯

2

◯ ◯ ☐ ◯ ◯
◯

Down + Distance	Yardline + –	L M R	Gain or Loss	Down + Distance	Yardline + –	L M R	Gain or Loss

3

◯ ◯ ☐ ◯ ◯
◯

4

◯ ◯ ☐ ◯ ◯
◯

DIAGRAM 9-1 Scouting Form

simple process that can easily be completed during halftime. Since each section of the scouting form is numbered
and each page is numbered (Diagram 9-1), scout #2 simply
says the section number and page number several times

during the process to make sure each is on the same play. After scout #2 verbally gives scout #1 the vital information (yard line, position on the field, down and distance, and gain or loss), scout #1 takes the booklet of scout #2 and records all line action in his booklet for each corresponding play.

Combining the information into one booklet is done to make the process of putting the information on the scouting charts much simpler. This process is again repeated at the conclusion of the game, prior to the actual breakdown of information.

When the game ends, the scouts analyze the information from the scouting booklets and put the information on the various scouting charts. Once this process is completed, the scouts begin to view the opponent's film. Scouting the film is a slightly different process from scouting an actual game. A film can be run back and forth, so there is no reason for three people to do the scouting. Normally only one is needed. He uses a Film Breakdown Form form for analyzing the film (Diagram 9-2).

The report on the game, viewed by the scout, is completed before scouting the film, so there is no real need to diagram every offensive play from the film. The only time a diagram is drawn is when the play is not seen in the scouted game or when the team runs a particular play in a slightly different manner in the film. Rather than diagramming every play, the name of the play is recorded in the space provided on the Film Breakdown Form. The play is named in the initial report of the actual game.

For example, when the following play (Diagram 9-3) was run in the scouted game, it was given the name "Option-Tight End Arc" in the scouting report and the abbreviation "Opt.-T.E. Arc" was used. When this play is viewed in the film, "Opt.-T.E. Arc," followed by the direction of the play, is recorded in the Play section of the Film Breakdown Form (Diagram 9-2).

Film Breakdown Form

PAGE

	Formation	Play	Defense	Down + Distance	Yardline + −	L M R	Gain or Loss
1	PRO.RT. I	OPT.-T.E. ARC-RT	5-2 CORNER	1-10	+48	M	+16
2							
3							
4							
5							
6							
7							
8							
9							

DIAGRAM 9-2 Film Breakdown Form

DIAGRAM 9-3

Another benefit from viewing the film is being able to record every defensive move employed by the opponent. This is very difficult to do during an actual game, but being able to run the film back and forth provides this information. A space is provided on the Film Breakdown Form to either diagram the defense or to describe it in words. After viewing the film and putting all the information on the Film Breakdown Forms, the information is analyzed and put on the scouting charts.

VARIOUS SCOUTING CHARTS

Because each scouting chart contains information from both the actual game and the film, the entries are put on the charts in different ways. Normally, one color pencil is used to record the game information and another color is used to record the film information. Another way to differentiate between the two sources of information is to draw a line between each source. This method is used in the diagrams illustrating the various scouting charts in this chapter. The information from the two sources is separated for analysis by the coach. This process gives the coach a quick view of both games at a glance.

Formation and Play

The Formation and Play Chart is the first one used in the analysis of game and film information. It has room for four formations on each chart. We have scouted opponents who use as many as thirty-two different formations, which requires eight Formation and Play Charts, and a few who use only one formation, which requires only one form (Diagram 9-4).

By looking at an individual block on the Formation and Play Chart, an explanation of its use is easily understood (Diagram 9-5). As the scout looks through the completed Backfield Defensive Scouting Booklet or the Film Breakdown Form, he looks at the first play and names the formation. He puts the name of the formation in the space provided. He then puts the abbreviated name of the play in the column in which it was run. Next to the abbreviated name of the play he puts the gain or loss. He then goes on to the next play. When the play is a pass, he lists the abbreviated name of the passing action used in the last column of the block. An example is "S. R." This abbreviations means "sprint pass to the right." The following is entered after the abbreviated name of the passing action:

1. When the pass is completed, the gain or loss is listed.
2. When the quarterback is sacked, "S" is followed by the loss in yardage.
3. When the quarterback keeps the ball and runs, "R" is followed by the gain in yardage.
4. When the pass is incomplete, "Inc." is recorded.
5. When the pass is intercepted, "Int." is recorded.

Any time a gain or loss is a result of a penalty, "P" follows the yardage. When the ball is lost as a result of a fumble, "F" is put after the gain or loss.

After completing the chart for the actual game and film, the scout lists next to the word "Frequency" the number of times the formation was used in the scouted game and in the film.

The following is some of the vital information that is acquired from this chart:

1. All the offensive formations used by the opponent.
2. The number of times each formation is used.

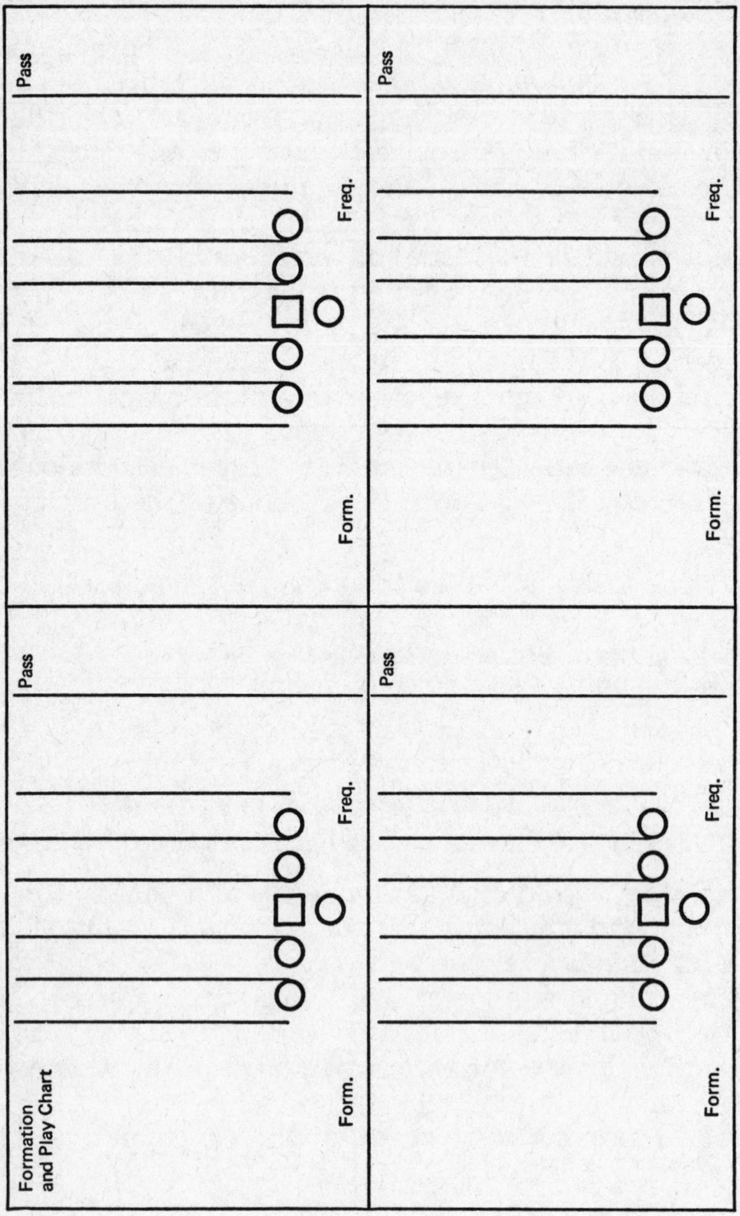

DIAGRAM 9-4 Formation and Play Chart

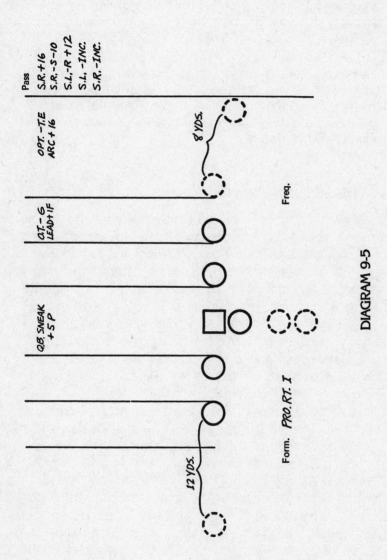

DIAGRAM 9-5

3. The plays the offense most uses in each formation.

4. The total number of times a team used a particular play. By adding the gains and losses, the total yardage for each play is also found. By dividing the number of times the play has been employed into the play's total yardage, the average gain per play is also acquired.

5. Not only are the number of times the various passing actions were used available, but the number of passes attempted, completed, intercepted, and the yardage lost and gained by the quarterback are also available at a glance.

Down and Distance, Field Position

This is actually three forms that comprise one chart. All three forms are the same except each one represents a different area of the field. Next to the word "Field Position," one form has "Right" for right hash mark, one has "Left" for left hash mark, and one has "Middle" for middle of the field. Each form lists various "Down and Distance" situations the areas the opponent can attack while running the ball, and an area for recording passes and kicks. There are also three special categories listed at the bottom of the form for plays used "Inside the 10-yard line," "Inside the 5-yard line," and "Extra Points" (Diagram 9-6).

As the scout again looks through the completed Backfield Defensive Scouting Booklet, he looks at the first play and checks the position on the field from which the play was run. He then selects the correct Down and Distance, Field Position Chart from "Right," "Left," or "Middle." Once he has the correct form, he looks back to the Backfield Defensive Scouting Booklet and finds the "Down and Distance." He then goes down the left-hand side of the form and locates the line on which the play should be written. He writes the name of the formation, the name of the play, and the gain or loss in the block under the correct area of attack.

FIELD POSITION: *RIGHT*

Down and Distance, Field Position Chart	L.E.	L.T.	L.G.	C	R.G.	R.T.	R.E.	Pass	Punts & Tricks
1 - 10									
1 - Less than 10									
1 - More than 10									
2 - 8 Yds. or More									
2 - 6 or 7 Yds.						{ PRO-RT. I / QT.G.LEAD +5			
2 - 5 Yds. or Less									
3 - 5 Yds or More									
3 - 3 or 4 Yds.									
3 - 2 Yds. or Less									
4 - 8 Yds. or More									
4 - 4 to 7 Yds.									
4 - 3 Yds. or Less									
Inside 10									
Inside 5									
X-Point									

DIAGRAM 9-6

The following is the actual procedure followed by the scout after viewing this block on the Scouting Form. (Diagram 9-7)

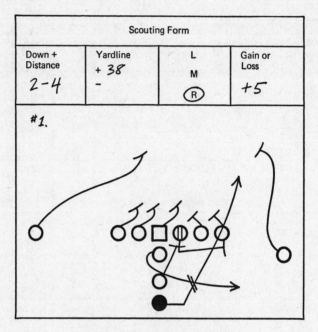

DIAGRAM 9-7 Scouting Form

1. He goes to the Down and Distance, Field Position Chart marked "Right."
2. He goes down the left-hand column and finds "2-5 yards or less."
3. He goes down the column marked "R.T." and locates the correct box.
4. He then prints an abbreviation for the formation. Since the formation is a pro-formation with an "I" backfield and the flanker to the right, he prints "Pro. Rt. I."
5. He writes an abbreviation for the play that he takes from the Formation and Play Chart. He prints "O.T-

G. lead." This means an off-tackle play with a guard lead-blocking at the point of attack.

6. He follows this with "+5," which is the amount of yardage gained.

The scout goes through the entire Backfield Defensive Scouting Booklet and categorizes every play and does the same with the Film Breakdown Form.

The following is some of the vital information that is acquired from the chart:

1. The plays and formations the opponent uses from the three positions on the field.

2. The plays and formations the opponent uses in all "Down and Distance" situations.

3. If the opponent has a tendency to employ plays that are designed to go to the sideline or to the open field.

4. The plays and formations that the opponent uses on the goal line.

Individual Pass and Run Summary

This chart is merely the plays from the Backfield Defensive Scouting Booklet and the Film Breakdown Form that are drawn neatly and accurately on a chart.

The first chart done is the Pass Summary Chart. This illustrates all the passing plays and shows the exact pass routes used and the depth at which the patterns are run. Below the play, the abbreviated name is given along with the number of times the play was run (Diagram 9-8).

The Run Summary Chart is then completed. This contains all the running plays that were employed by the opponent. Like the Pass Summary Chart, it also contains the abbreviated name of each play as well as the number of time each was run in the game and the film (Diagram 9-9).

The purpose of this chart is to give the coach a quick look at every play the opponent used in the previous two games and the number of times each play was used. The coach takes this chart and draws the plays on "5 x 8" index

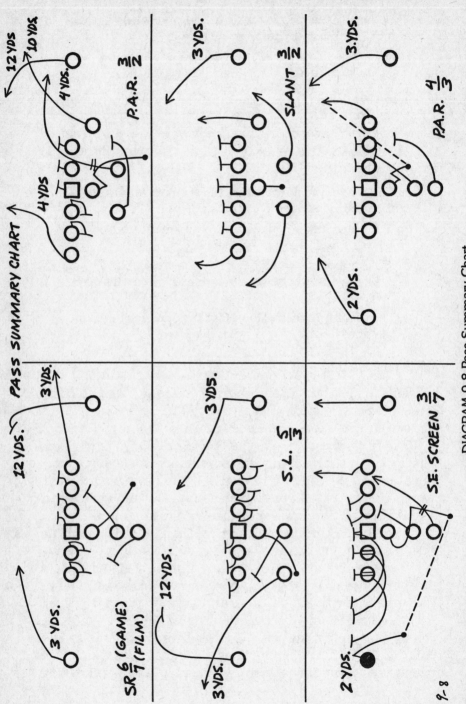

DIAGRAM 9-8 Pass Summary Chart

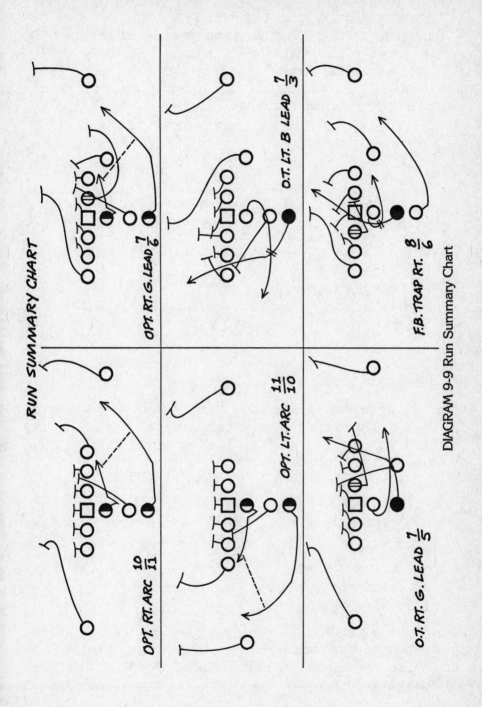

RUN SUMMARY CHART

OPT. RT. ARC $\frac{10}{11}$

OPT. LT. ARC $\frac{11}{10}$

OPT. RT. G. LEAD $\frac{7}{6}$

O.T. LT. B LEAD $\frac{7}{3}$

O.T. RT. G. LEAD $\frac{7}{5}$

F.B. TRAP RT. $\frac{8}{6}$

DIAGRAM 9-9 Run Summary Chart

cards. These are Scout Team Play Cards and are used by the scout team coach during the week. He shows them to the scout team and they run the plays against the defensive team. The Scout Team Play Cards are covered in plastic so they will remain usable in bad weather and can be saved for future reference (Diagram 9-10).

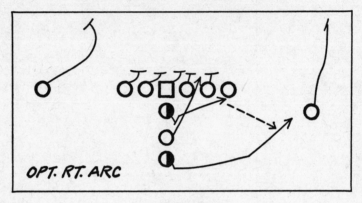

OPT. RT. ARC

DIAGRAM 9-10

Offensive Personnel

The Offensive Personnel Chart contains the names of all the players who played on offense for the opponent in either the game or the film. The following information is given on each player:

1. Number
2. Position
3. Height
4. Weight
5. Class in school
6. Strengths
7. Weaknesses

This chart is done primarily by scout #3. It is his responsibility to watch personnel during the game, and he is also responsible to evaluate personnel from the film (Diagram 9-11).

Offensive Personnel Chart Name	Number	Position	Height	Weight	Class	Strengths	Weaknesses
DOE, JOHN	7	QB	6'3"	190	JR.	VERY QUICK FEET GOOD PASSER	
SMITH, BILL	32	FB	5'11"	218	SR.	CO-CAPTAIN STRONG	POOR SPEED
JONES, RON	22	TB	5'9"	165	SO.	EXCEPTIONAL SPEED	FUMBLES
KENT, TOM	25	FLK.	6'3"	170	SR.	GOOD HANDS	POOR BLOCKER
ADAMS, BOB	88	T.E.	6'0"	203	SR.	EXCELLENT BLOCKER	POOR RECEIVER
JENKINS, RAY	78	R.T	6'4"	245	JR.		POOR PASS BLOCKER
GUYER, BILL	65	R.G.	5'11"	190	SO.		SLOW
COOMBS, FRED	51	C	6'3"	210	SR.	VERY QUICK	
TURNER, JOE	60	L.G.	6'0"	180	SR.	CO-CAPTAIN BEST BLOCKER	
FRY, AMOS	75	L.T	6'5"	230	JR.		OFTEN HOLDS
KEENE, JACK	91	S.E	5'7"	145	SO.	BEST RECEIVER VERY QUICK	POOR BLOCKER
(SUBSTITUTE) BUNCE, TONY	20	T.B.	5'9"	165	SR.		POOR PASS BLOCKER
(SUBSTITUTE) KURTS, BILLY	77	L.T.	6'6"	210	SR.		POOR PASS BLOCKER

DIAGRAM 9-11 Offensive Personnel Chart

After all the charts are completed, the scouts present the complete report to the coaching staff along with any other information they feel will be helpful. After viewing the opponent's film, the staff is ready to prepare the Defensive Game Plan.

COORDINATING THE SCOUTING REPORT AND THE DEFENSIVE GAME PLAN

The coaches first look at the Formation and Play Chart and determine if the opponent has a formation tendency. When an opponent has a strong formation tendency, then it is determined to use a particular defense automatically versus that formation. This *Automatic Defense* is automatic no matter what was called in the defensive huddle. The left linebacker and the safety are responsible for recognition of the formation as well as calling the Automatic Defense on the ball. The following are a few reasons why an Automatic Defense may be used against a particular formation:

1. The opponent has attacked only one or two areas along the offensive front as opposed to attacking all areas.

2. The opponent has attacked all areas along the offensive front but has attacked one or two areas much more than the others.

3. The opponent has only passed or only run from the formation.

4. The opponent has employed only inside or only outside running plays from the formation.

Once the coaching staff decides on an Automatic Defense (or Automatic Defenses), it is listed at the top of the Defensive Game Plan Ready Sheet.

The coaches next look at the Down and Distance, Field Position Chart and determine what tendencies the opponent has shown in these areas. These tendencies, unlike formation tendencies, are not handled by Automatic Defenses. Suppose, for example, that the opponent indicates a strong tendency toward a particular formation when in a certain part of the field and on a specific down and distance. A defense to handle this situation would then be made part of the Game Plan, and the coach would call the defense in this particular Down and Distance, Field Position situation. When the opponent has not shown a tendency in a particular situation, the defensive coach calls defenses that he feels suit the situation and will cause confusion for the opponent.

The Combination-60 Defense is designed so that all defenses are balanced and can handle all offensive situations. Therefore, there are really no wrong calls. There are simply some defenses that are better than others in particular situations.

The coaches finally look at the Offensive Personnel Chart and determine if any individual offensive player requires particular defensive attention. The following are some situations that indicate particular defensive adjustments:

1. When a team has a particularly weak offensive lineman, it may be decided to play a defensive lineman in an "Up" technique on him to take advantage of his weakness.

2. When a team has an exceptional wide receiver, a possible adjustment is to play the offside linebacker or the onside end in a Double-Up on him in passing situations.

3. When a team runs the option and the quarterback is an exceptional runner, it may be decided to double-cover the quarterback on all option plays.

The Defensive Game Plan Ready Sheet is similar to the Down and Distance, Field Position Chart in that it has particular Down and Distance situations down the left-hand side. It is divided into the three areas of the field as far as the offensive team is concerned: the right, left and middle sections. Where it has been decided to use a defense in a particular Down and Distance, Field Position situation, the defense is listed in that box and will be called when that situation arises during the game.

Even though the coaches actually call the defenses, copies of the plan are given to the left linebackers and safeties so they can develop a feeling for what will be called. This also gives them the opportunity to see the Automatic Defenses (Diagram 9-12).

Upon completion of the Defensive Game Plan Ready Sheet, the coaches make up a Scouting Report for the players. It is a brief summary of the opponent's strengths and weaknesses, as well as diagrams of those plays they most often employ. It contains a summary of the Defensive Game Plan, but is not nearly as complete as the Defensive Game Plan Ready Sheet. These are given to the defensive players on Monday, prior to practice, and are collected on Thursday, after practice. The players are then given a wirtten quiz on the Scouting Report. The quiz simply tests the players' knowledge of the opponent as well as their understanding of the Game Plan. This has proven to be an excellent tool to encourage the defensive personnel to study their Scouting Reports.

ADJUSTING THE DEFENSIVE GAME PLAN DURING THE GAME

During a game there are two kinds of adjustments that can be made. There are adjustments in the Game Plan and personnel adjustments.

A coach is positioned in the press box. His responsibility is to determine if the opponent is showing the same tendencies that were shown in the game and film that were scouted. He does this by using a Film Breakdown Form and by scouting the opponent. When the opponent no longer has the ball, the coach compares the information he has just recorded with the Formation and Play and Down and Distance, Field Position Charts. When the opponent shows different tendencies from those on the charts, the information is immediately given to the coach who is responsible for the defensive calls, and any desired adjustments in the Defensive Game Plan are made. Most often,

Automatic Defenses:
1. VS. PRO. RT. I   "SLANT LT." – "CORNER"
2. VS. PRO LT. I   "UP RT" – "M/M"

Defensive Game Plan Ready Sheet	Automatic Defenses		
	Left	Middle	Right
1 - 10	"SLANT LT." – "INVERT"		
1 - Less than 10			
1 - More than 10.	"SLANT - GUARDS UP-RT" "M/M"		
2 - 8 Yds. or More			"SLANT-TACKLES UP. RIGHT - "M/M"
2 - 6 or 7 Yds.			
2 - 5 Yds. or Less	"SLANT-RT" – "CORNER"	"SLANT-RT" – "CORNER"	
3 - 5 Yds. or More		"TOUGH"-"M/M"	"UP-RT." "INVERT"
3 - 3 or 4 Yds.			
3 - 2 Yds. or Less	"GAP" – "M/M"	"SLANT-OUT" –"M/M	
4 - 8 Yds. or More	"UP-LT." "FREE SAFETY PREVENT"	"UP-LT" – "FREE SAFETY LOCK-ON S.E."	
4 - 4 to 7 Yds.			
4 - 3 Yds. or Less			
Inside 10			
Inside 5	"GAP" – "M/M"	"TOUGH" – "M/M"	"SLANT-IN" – "M/M"
X - Point			

DIAGRAM 9-12 Defensive Game Plan Ready Sheet

the adjustments are made at halftime, since the coach who is charting the opponent has had a full half to accumulate information and determine tendencies. This also gives the entire defensive staff an opportunity to analyze the information and decide upon any desired alterations in the game plan.

The second type of game adjustment is for personnel reasons. These changes are determined by the coach in the press box, the coach on the field, and the individual players. The following are the most common changes:

1. When a defensive lineman is having trouble reaching his target point, it may be decided that he should use his "Up" technique or his Cheat Adjustment rather than "Slanting."

2. When it is discovered that an offensive lineman is weak and cannot handle the defensive lineman, it may be decided to always play a defensive lineman "Up" on him, rather than "Slanting" to him.

3. If the opponent is throwing slant passes to a wide receiver, the onside end or the outside linebacker could be instructed to play either a Walkaway or a Double-Up to the side of the receiver.

POST-GAME EVALUATION

There are three phases to this post-game evaluation procedure:

1. The individual defensive personnel
2. The Defensive Game Plan
3. The performance of our opponent

Prior to the Sunday evening staff meeting, each coach views the game film and grades the performances of the defensive players for whom he is responsible. The grades are discussed at the staff meeting and it is decided if any changes are needed in the defensive lineup.

At the staff meeting the coaching staff views the game film together to determine the effectiveness of the Defensive Game Plan. The following questions are discussed and the answers are recorded for future reference:

1. If we were going to play the same opponent next week, what changes should be made in the Game Plan?
2. Were the adjustments, if any, made during the game effective?
3. What adjustments, if any, should have been made during the game that were not made?
4. What was our most effective defense? Why?
5. What was our least effective defense? Why?

A manager keeps a record during the game of each defensive call and the gain or loss by the opponent on each play. This helps answer questions 4 and 5.

The evaluation of the opponent's performance is done as a preparation for next year's game. This information, along with the evaluation of our Defensive Game Plan, is filed with all the information we have developed on the opponent over the years. The Formation and Play and Down and Distance, Field Position charts are completed by adding our game to those of the opponent. This three-game report is brought to the staff meeting. The following questions concerning our game are discussed and the answers recorded for future reference:

1. Where did they hurt us?
2. Did they do anything different from what we had expected?
3. Does the opponent have any sophomores or juniors who caused us problems?

On Monday evening, the team views the game film and any necessary comments concerning the game are then made.

THE COMBINATION-60 DRILLS AND DEFENSIVE PRACTICE SCHEDULE

10

The Combination-60 practice schedule is somewhat unique in that the team practices only three days a week. The three practice days are Tuesday, Wednesday, and Thursday.

On Monday afternoon the team receives their Scouting Reports on the upcoming opponents. The junior varsity players then have a J.V. game while the varsity players go through a short weight training and rope jumping program. After this workout, the varsity players are free to go to the J.V. game. On Monday evening, there is a team meeting (both varsity and junior varsity) to review Saturday's game and to discuss the upcoming opponent, and to go over the Scouting Report.

On Friday evening there is a team meeting in the gymnasium. The team goes through some stretching exercises. The various teams (offense, defense, and specialty) are reviewed so each player is sure of his Game Day responsibilities, and each coach meets with his area of responsibility to answer any last-minute questions.

Saturday is Game Day for the varsity. The junior varsity players meet prior to the game and go through the short weight training and rope jumping program.

The Tuesday, Wednesday, and Thursday practice schedule is the same every week. It is posted the first week of the season and never changes. This allows the players to be fully aware of what to expect at practice and thus eliminates any fear of the unknown.

The practice schedule (Diagram 10-1) is divided into various periods. Each period has a specific purpose and each drill within the period serves that purpose. Many of the basic tackling and ball drills that are used with most defensive systems are also employed in the Combination-60 practice plan. However, the drills described in this chapter are either wholly or partially unique to the Combination-60 or are basic defensive drills that are employed every day during practice without variation. For simplicity's sake, "O" represents offensive players and "X" represents defensive players in all drill diagrams in this chapter.

STRETCH PERIOD

During this period various stretching exercises are performed to loosen the players and to help prevent injuries. The coaches pay particularly close attention to each player to be sure each one is performing the exercises correctly. Unless these exercises are done in a very strict fashion, they are of little value in the prevention of muscle pulls and other injuries. The stretching drills are lead by the team co-captains who are in the middle of the stretch formation. The coaches align behind their own position area of responsibility and watch and guide their own players (Diagram 10-2).

INDIVIDUAL PERIOD

This period is divided into four, five-minute intervals. During this period, members of the individual defensive areas (linebackers and ends, line and secondary) work

PRACTICE SCHEDULE

TIME (Minutes) Periods	Tues.	Weds.	Thurs.	LINE	Linebackers & Ends	
Stretch	10	10	10			
Individual	20	20	20	1. Dummy Wave (2 min.) 2. Shiver Slide (3 min.) 3. Hose Attack (5 min.) 4. Sled Attack (5 min.) 5. Tackling Drills (5 min.)	1. Leverage Drill (5 min.) 2. Read and Step (5 min.) 3. Turn and Catch (2 min.) 4. Down the Line (3 min.) 5. Tackling Drills (5 min.)	1. Shuffle, Peddle (5 min.) 2. Turn and Catch (2 min.) 3. Down the Line (3 min.) 4. Receiving Drills (5 min.) 5. Tackling Drills (5 min.)
1st Kicking	15	15	10			
Teaching	10	0	0			
Group	20	20	20	1. Technique and Recognition (10 min.) 2. Stop The Run (10 min.)	1. Man To Man Drills (10 min.) 2. Stop The Run / Wave - Flow } 10 min.	1. Man To Man Drills (10 min.) 2. Wave - Flow (10 min.)
Halftime	5	5	5			
Combo	20	20	20	1. One On One (10 min.) 2. Live Rush (10 min.)	7 on 7 / Skeleton	7 on 7 / Skeleton
Team	20	25	10	1. Power Drill (10 min.)	1. Power Drill (10 min.)	1. Power Drill (10 min.)
2nd Kicking	10	10	5			
Weight Lifting Rope Jumping	0	0	45			

DIAGRAM 10-1 Practice Schedule

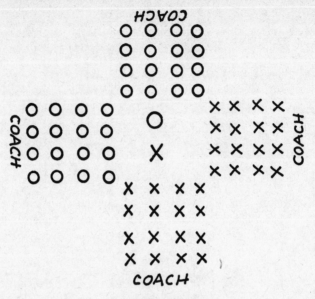

DIAGRAM 10-2

with the members of their area to develop the individual skills that are needed for the success of the Combination-60.

Defensive Line

The defensive line works on the development of quick feet and a good hand shiver. They perfect their various attack techniques ("Slant," "Up," "Gap," "Tough") and work on proper tackling.

Dummy Wave

Equipment: Four long dummies.

Purpose: To develop quick feet, balance, and agility.

Time: Two minutes.

Four defensive linemen align facing the coach, each straddling a dummy. The dummies are 1 yard apart. On the command of the coach, they step over the dummies while constantly facing the coach. The coach gives the direction he wants the players to move by pointing in that direction.

This forces the linemen to keep their heads up while performing the drill. The linemen stay in a low breakdown position as they perform the drill. When the coach yells "pass," the linemen sprint to the coach with their hands up, as if they were rushing a passer. Upon completion, they go to the back of the four lines and another group performs the drill. The coach gives each group at least four direction changes while they are performing the drill.

Coaching Points: The players must move quickly, while maintaining a good low position with the heads up and facing forward. The players must also use high-knee action (Diagram 10-3).

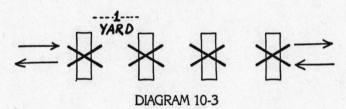

DIAGRAM 10-3

Shiver slide

Equipment: Seven-man sled.

Purpose: To develop a good hand shiver and quick feet.

Time: Three minutes.

The defensive linemen align one behind another, facing forward, at one end of the seven-man sled. On the command of the coach, the first lineman proceeds to hand shiver the first sled pad. Then he bounces off that pad and proceeds to attack each pad. He forms another line at the other end of the sled after attacking all seven pads. The second lineman does not start until the first defender hits the third sled pad. This eliminates the possibility of one lineman hitting another. When the defensive linemen go to the right, they use the right foot when attacking the sled. When they go to the left, they use the left foot. The linemen stay in a breakdown position with their heads up and facing forward while executing the drill. After all linemen complete one turn down the sled, they go again in the opposite direction. Depending on the number of defensive linemen, they should go up and back at least four times during the three-minute period.

Coaching Points: The players must lock their elbows on contact with the sled. The players cannot sacrifice good technique for speed. Their speed through the drill is not nearly as important as a good hand shiver. They use short, choppy steps and never cross their feet (Diagram 10-4).

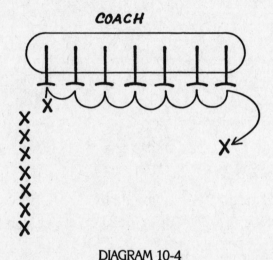

DIAGRAM 10-4

Hose Attack

Equipment: One fire hose painted to represent the offensive line with normal splits, one football.

Purpose: To develop the proper alignment, foot movement, body position, quickness, and the proper pursuit angles, while executing the various attacks.

Time: Five minutes.

A defensive line forms a huddle and awaits the defensive call by the coach. After the call, they break the huddle and align on one knee in their proper positions on the ball. When the coach puts his hand on the ball, they assume a three-point stance. As the coach moves the ball, the line executes the proper techniques. After the initial movement of the ball, the coach waves the ball to either the right or the left. The linemen get into the proper angle of pursuit and sprint until the coach puts the ball on the ground. Having the coach maintain possession of the ball during the entire drill forces the linemen to face the coach until the drill is completed. This teaches the defenders to never pursue blindly but to always know the location of the ball.

Coaching Points: The players must stay in a good, low position and move as quickly as possible. Even though they are not going against any players, they must still execute the hand shiver when they are "Slanting" and a forearm shiver when using "Up" or "Tough." They must go full speed at all times, and this must be emphasized during pursuit (Diagram 10-5).

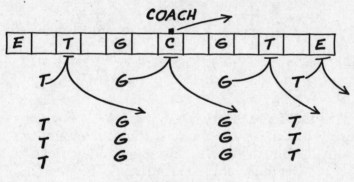

DIAGRAM 10-5

Sled Attack

Equipment: Seven-man sled, one football.

Purpose: To develop the same qualities as Hose Attack, with the addition of hitting techniques.

Time: Five minutes.

This drill is done in the same manner as Hose Attack, except that the players actually execute their hand and forearm shivers on the sled. After the players make contact with the sled, the coach moves the ball for the pursuit angle. This drill combines the movement of Hose Attack, the hand-shiver technique of Shiver Slide, and the agility of Dummy Wave.

> *Coaching Points:* Since this drill is a combination of the first three drills, the players must put together all the qualities and techniques they learned and practiced in those drills (Diagram 10-6).

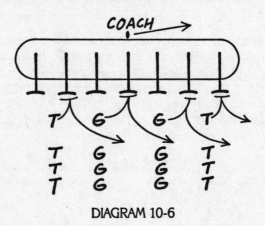

DIAGRAM 10-6

The last five-minute interval is used for various basic tackling drills. Unlike the first three intervals, the drills used in this interval differ from day to day and add some variety to the daily practice routine.

Linebackers and Ends

During this period, like the linemen, the linebackers and the ends work on quick feet and good balance. They work to develop a good forearm shiver and work to perfect their ability to read the movement of the offensive players. They also practice their tackling techniques.

Leverage Drill

Equipment: Two-man sled, four hand-held dummies, two footballs.

Purpose: To develop a good forearm shiver, quick feet, good balance, and the ability to keep outside leverage on the ball.

Time: Five minutes.

The players split into two equal groups. Each group forms a line facing forward, one behind the other, on a sled pad. The first defender in each line aligns as tight to the sled as possible. The linebackers use their basic parallel stance and the ends align in their normal stance, with their outside foot back. When the coach gives the command, the first player in each group steps with his inside foot and attacks the sled with his inside forearm. Each player continues to the outside, where he meets two blockers with shields, one after another, who attempt to keep the defenders from getting outside. The first blocker is 2 yards outside the sled and the second blocker is 2 yards outside the first. The blockers attack the defenders high or low while the defenders attack the blockers with their inside forearms and push them to the inside with their outside free arms. After contact is completed with the second blocker, the defenders attack the ballcarrier who is running from behind the sled to the outside. The defenders do not tackle the ballcarrier but make high body contact with him, keeping their heads to the outside while wrapping their arms around the ballcarrier. Upon completion of the drill, the defenders switch lines. Each player should go through each line twice, hold both shields, and also be a ballcarrier.

Coaching Points: The players cannot cross their feet during this drill. They must slide down the line in a good, low football position. The players must not give ground to the blockers but must operate along the line of scrimmage. The ballcarrier runs under controlled speed to allow the defenders to make good contact with the blockers before getting to the outside too quickly, without getting enough work on the forearm shiver (Diagram 10-7).

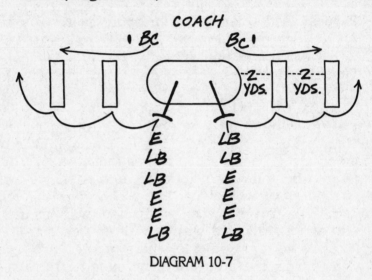

DIAGRAM 10-7

Read and step

Equipment: One football, one fire hose painted to represent the offensive line.

Purpose:

1. To teach the ends to take their proper steps and to teach the onside end to react to various inside situations.

2. To teach the linebackers to take the correct first step according to the movements of their offensive keys.

Time: Five minutes.

Four defenders align as offensive players on the hose. One aligns as a center, two as tight ends, and the fourth as a back or a guard to the side of the defensive call. Two linebackers and two ends align on the ball according to the defensive call. The coach stands behind the defenders and, with hand signals, gives the offensive players directions as to the snap count and what he wants them to do. The linebackers, on the movement of the ball by the center, react to the movements of their keys by taking their first step. The center can do the following: (1) fire straight out; (2) pass block; (3) step down the line to either side; (4) step toward either imaginary defensive guard. The tight end to the side of the offside linebacker can do the following: (1) fire straight out; (2) attempt an inside or outside pass release; (3) pass block; (4) step inside or outside to block.

The ends then take their normal steps as the ball is snapped. The offside end executes a Pinch technique on the tight end. The onside end takes his three-step shuffle and looks to the inside and reacts according to the movement of the inside offensive player. The inside offensive player can do the following: (1) align as a back and attack the end; (2) align as a back and dive; (3) align as a back and pass block; (4) align as a guard and attack the end; (5) align as a guard and block straight ahead.

The coach is careful to coordinate the movement of the tight end, to the side of the onside end, and the inside offensive player. If this were not done, an unnatural situation could arise. An example of this is when the tight end attempts to arc block the onside end while the guard is also pulling to block him. During the drill, the ends and linebackers play both onside and offside.

Coaching Points: The players must totally concentrate on their keys and react to their movement and not be concerned with any other facet of the drill. For this reason, no ballcarrier is included in the drill (Diagram 10-8).

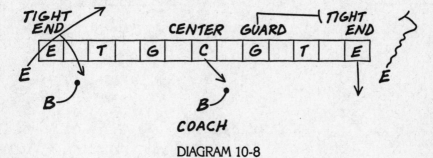

DIAGRAM 10-8

Turn and catch

Equipment: Four footballs.
Purpose: To improve the defender's ability to react to
the football, catch it, tuck it away, and run
with it. This drill also teaches concentration
on the football.
Time: Two minutes.

The players split into two equal groups about 20 yards
apart. Each group forms a line, one behind the other,
while facing the front. A coach stands 10 yards in front of
one line while facing the line and a manager does the same
in front of the other line. On the command of the coach,
the first player turns his back to the coach (manager) and
awaits a verbal command to turn and catch the ball. The
coach (manager) gives the verbal command once the ball
has been thrown.

The player must locate the ball and catch it. He then
tucks it away and sprints to the passer (coach or manager)
and puts the ball down at his side. The player then goes to
the back of the opposite line.

Coaching Points: The players must look the ball into
their hands and catch it before they attempt to sprint
to the passer. They must be careful to carry the ball
correctly as they return the ball (Diagram 10-9).

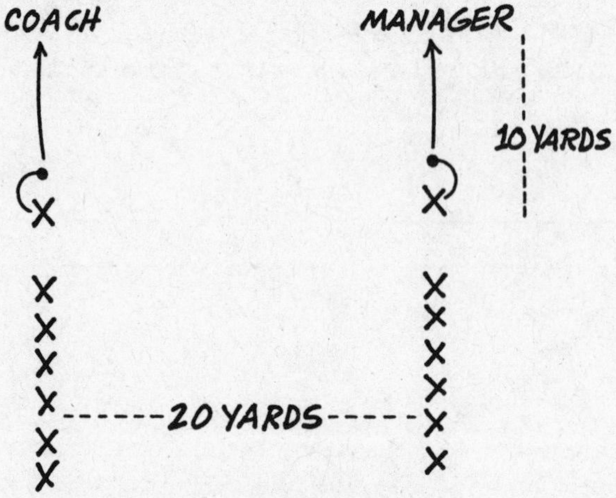

DIAGRAM 10-9

Down the line

Equipment: Four footballs.
Purpose: Same as Turn and Catch.
Time: Three minutes.

The initial alignment of the defenders is the same as Turn and Catch, except that they are 20 yards from the coach (manager). The coach (manager) slaps the ball and the first player in each line sprints toward him. The coach (manager) passes the ball to the player who catches it, tucks it away, and sprints to the coach to return the ball. Like Turn and Catch, the player then goes to the back of the opposite line. At first, the coach (manager) passes the ball directly to the player. As the drill progresses, the ball is passed in such a way that the player must extend himself to catch it.

> *Coaching Points:* The players must extend themselves to catch the ball and keep the same concentration they learned in Turn and Catch. The other coaching points are the same as Turn and Catch.

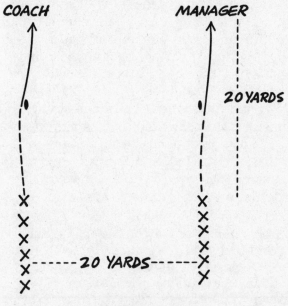

DIAGRAM 10-10

Like the defensive linemen, the linebackers and end do various basic tackling drills in the last five-minute interval of the individual period (Diagram 10-10).

Secondary

This period is devoted to the development of quick feet, good balance, and the ability to catch the football. Like the other defensive areas, tackling is also worked on in the fourth five-minute interval.

Shuffle, peddle

Equipment: One football.
Purpose: To teach the correct shuffle steps and develop the ability to backpeddle while keeping complete control of the body.
Time: Five minutes.

Two equal groups are formed 5 yards apart. They align in the same fashion as Turn and Catch, with the coach in front of and between the two lines with his back to the line. On the command of the coach, a player from each line goes to a position 5 yards in front of the coach and 10 yards apart. They align in their correct stances. The defensive halfbacks align as left halfbacks when they are in the left line and right halfbacks when they are in the right line. When the coach raises the ball over his head, the players execute their shuffle steps, then backpeddle until the coach puts the ball to the right or left. The players push off the correct foot and sprint in the direction of the ball. They sprint until the coach throws the ball. One player intercepts the ball and the other acts as a blocker. They sprint to the back of the opposite line after the interception and await another turn.

Coaching Points: The players must execute the shuffle steps and backpeddle in a good, low football position. When the players change direction and sprint in the direction of the ball, they must not cross their feet but open step in the direction they are going. The players

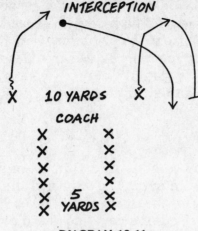

DIAGRAM 10-11

must also keep their eyes on the ball at all times (Diagram 10-11).

During the second five-minute interval, the secondary perform the Turn and Catch and Down the Line drills. The third five-minute interval is devoted to any basic ballcatching drills that the coach wishes to employ. The fourth interval is devoted to various tackling drills.

FIRST KICKING PERIOD

During this period, the offensive and defensive teams come together. The offensive team works on punting, extra points, and field goals while the defensive unit works on the defense for these phases of the game. Particular attention is paid to the punt return since it acts as a conditioning part of practice. Every member of the defensive team is on a punt return team and the coaches make very sure that every player sprints at top speed during the punt return segment of the period.

TEACHING PERIOD

This period is used only on Tuesday. During this period the Defensive Game Plan is put in with each

individual area and any Automatics or special defensive
plans are practiced. This period provides the time for the
coaches to implement the plans that were discussed in the
Monday evening meeting. It also provides a period of time
for the players to get all questions concerning the Game
Plan answered and straight in their minds.

GROUP PERIOD

This period is split into two, ten-minute intervals.
During the first interval, the offensive and defensive lines
work together and the linebackers and ends work with the
secondary and some offensive backs and receivers. During
the second interval, half of the linebackers and ends work
with the defensive line while the other half works with the
secondary. After five minutes, the group with the defensive line goes with the secondary, and the group with the
secondary goes with the defensive line. This period develops interaction between the various defensive areas and
begins to coordinate the entire defensive team.

Defensive Line

This period provides an opportunity for defensive
linemen to see and react to the various blocking schemes
of the upcoming opponent. It also provides time for the
defensive line to work with the linebackers and ends
against the opponent's running game.

Technique and recognition

Equipment: Two footballs.
Purpose: To develop the various attack techniques
against actual people and to recognize the
various blocking schemes of the offensive
line.
Time: Ten minutes.

The defensive line is split into two groups. One group
consists of the defensive guards and the other group is the

defensive tackles. An offensive center, two offensive guards, and an offensive tackle are sent with the defensive guards. An offensive center, offensive tackle, and tight end are sent with the defensive tackles. The groups are 10 yards apart with the coach in the middle behind the defensive players. From this position he can give the offensive players hand signals to indicate the various blocking schemes he wants executed as well as the snap count.

The offensive linemen align as a right offensive line for one-half of the drill and a left offensive line for the other half of the drill. This allows the defensive linemen to play both right and left at their position.

The defensive linemen execute the technique that was called by the coach (example: "Slant-Right") on the movement of the ball. As they execute their technique, they recognize the various blocking schemes and react accordingly. This drill is executed at top speed and live contact is expected.

> *Coaching Points:* The linemen must execute their techniques properly in a good, low position and make sure they keep themselves square to the line of scrimmage. As the linemen recognize the blocking scheme, they must react accordingly. For example, when the guard recognizes a trap, he must step into the trapping guard and prevent a hole from developing (Diagram 10-12).

COACH

DIAGRAM 10-12

Stop the Run

Equipment: One football.
Purpose: To bring the defensive linemen together

with the linebacker and ends and to have the entire group execute their various techniques against a scout team that is using the opponent's running plays.

Time: Ten minutes.

A defensive front (defensive linemen, linebackers, and ends) form a defensive huddle, call the defense, and align over the ball on one knee, awaiting the offensive team. An entire scout team comes over the ball and runs the opponent's plays. Every aspect is live except tackling. The defenders are to hit the ballcarrier chest high and wrap their arms but not take the ballcarrier to the ground. The linebacker and end coach and the defensive line coach stand behind the defense while the scout team coach runs the offensive.

Coaching Points: The defenders must move on the snap of the ball and execute the proper techniques. This drill is designed to teach the defenders to get to the right place rather than making the tackle. The defenders must also get into the correct paths of pursuit.

Linebackers and Ends

This period provides an opportunity for the linebackers and the ends to work with both the defensive line and the secondary. It also provides time to work on man-to-man coverage as well as zone drops. During the first ten-minute interval, the linebackers and ends work with the secondary and perform basic man-to-man coverage drills against scout team receivers and backs.

Wave-Flow

Equipment: Two footballs, one fire hose painted to represent the offensive line with normal splits, two cones.

Purpose: To teach the secondary, linebackers, and ends to take the proper angle versus runs and passes and to react to the ball when thrown.

Time: Ten minutes.

During this drill, half the linebackers and ends are with the defensive line performing the Stop and Run Drill, and half are with the secondary. After five minutes the groups switch.

A defensive group properly aligns on the hose and the cones (cones represent wide receivers). The coach aligns behind the hose as a quarterback. When he smacks the ball, the secondary performs their shuffle and the defensive ends perform their techniques. He then does one of the following five things with the ball:

1. He lifts it straight over his head. This represents a dropback pass.
2. He lifts the ball high to the right or left. This represents a wide passing action.
3. He puts the ball to the right or left. This represents a run to the right or left.

The defensive players react according to the front and secondary call that was made in the huddle. The players continue movement until the coach throws the ball after holding it to indicate a pass. The defender who intercepts it yells "Bingo," and all other defenders must get in a position to block for him. The coach blows the whistle after putting the ball in a position to indicate the run. The linebacker and end coach acts as the quarterback. The secondary coach stands behind the secondary.

Coaching Points: The players must react to the movement of the football and stay in a good, low football position. Since the linebackers do not have a key to read, they simply chop their feet until the coach moves the ball in some direction. When the ball is smacked, the linebackers begin to chop. *All* players must go for the ball when it is thrown, and block the ball after it is intercepted (Diagram 10-13).

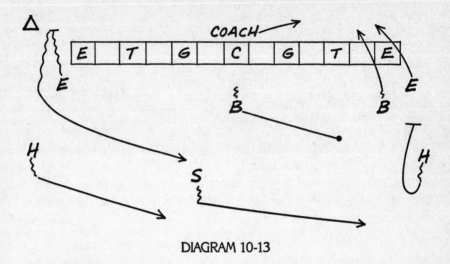

DIAGRAM 10-13

Secondary

This period allows the secondary to work on man-to-man drills and work with the linebackers and ends on various pass coverages. During the first ten-minute interval, the secondary execute man-to-man drills with the linebackers and ends. During the second ten-minute interval, the secondary performs the Wave-Flow Drill with the linebackers and the ends.

HALFTIME

During this five-minute period, the entire defense is allowed to rest and take all the ice and water they wish. It is actually a rest period. During the entire practice the players are allowed to take water and ice as long as it does not interfere with practice.

COMBO

This period is primarily concerned with defending against the pass. During this period, the secondary works with the linebackers, ends, scout receivers, ballcarriers, and quarterback in a seven-skeleton drill for the entire 20 minutes.

Defensive Line

During this period the defensive line works on recognition of the pass block as well as the various methods of rushing the passer.

One-on-One

Equipment: Four long dummies.
Purpose: To develop individual rush techniques.
Time: Ten minutes.

Two dummies are put on the ground 2 yards apart and parallel to each other. This is called an *alley*. An offensive lineman assumes his position at the top and between the two dummies. A defensive lineman aligns head on the offensive player. The coach stands behind the defensive players. The offensive player moves when he wishes and begins to pass block. The defensive lineman attacks the blocker and fights to get beyond the other end of the dummies as quickly as possible. Normally two alleys are used to allow more players to participate.

Coaching Points: The defensive players must use the basic pass rush techniques and work as hard and quickly as possible (Diagram 10-14).

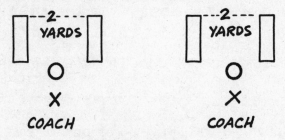

DIAGRAM 10-14

Live Rush

Equipment: One football.
Purpose: To work on the proper line techniques as well as a good pass rush.
Time: Ten minutes.

An entire defensive line forms a huddle and the coach calls a front defense. The front aligns on the ball, awaiting the offense. The scout team coach forms a huddle with an offensive scout team that consists of two guards, two tackles, and a center. The coach acts as the quarterback and calls for a dropback pass right, pass left, or screen. He takes the team to the line, calls the signals, and takes the ball from the center. He then executes the action he called in the huddle. The defensive linemen execute their techniques and attack the coach. Of course, they only grab him and do not tackle him, even though they may want to tackle him. The defensive line coach stands behind the defensive line.

Coaching Points: The defensive linemen must execute their techniques properly and then rush the quarterback.

TEAM

This period brings the entire defensive unit together to scrimmage the offensive scout team. On Tuesday and Thursday, they scrimmage only Gap and Tough and any other defenses that are going to be used on the goal line. On Wednesday, they scrimmage the entire Defensive Game Plan.

On Tuesday, the offense joins the defense for the first ten minutes of Team Defense and together they execute the Power Drill.

Power Drill

Equipment: Two 10-yard hoses, one football.
Purpose: To teach the defenders to make good contact with blockers and then make good tackles. It also works to teach the offensive linemen good blocking techniques and the offensive backs good running techniques. It is a real "toughness" drill for both the offense and defense.
Time: Ten minutes.

The two hoses are put on the ground 8 yards apart and parallel to each other. An offensive center and two linemen align at one end of the hoses facing the other end. They are 2 yards apart. A back aligns 3 yards deep behind each blocker (not the center) and a quarterback aligns under the center. A defender aligns head on each blocker. It can be a defensive lineman, member of the secondary, a linebacker, or an end. The coach stands behind the defensive unit and gives the starting count with hand signals to the offense, and indicates which running back will get the ball.

Both running backs run-dive and the quarterback gives the ball to the designated runner. The blockers attempt to block the defenders away from the hole. For the offense to score, they must go 10 yards in three downs. The defense must stop them in order to score. This drill develops a great deal of spirit and is very competitive (Diagram 10-15).

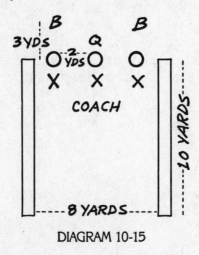

DIAGRAM 10-15

SECOND KICKING PERIOD

During this period the defense works on the kickoff. Every member of the defensive unit is on the kickoff team and this provides an excellent conditioning time at the end of practice.

ROPE JUMPING AND WEIGHT LIFTING

This is done on Monday and Thursday by the varsity and on Thursday and Saturday by the junior varsity. Thursday's practice is cut short so this period can be added. On Thursday, the entire team goes through the rope jumping and weight program. At most, this period takes 45 minutes and has proven to be well worth the time used.

Before we incorporated these two periods into our weekly practice schedule, the players lifted weights and jumped rope from the beginning of January until the start of practice in August. When the players began working in January, their performances were far below those of late August. They had lost some of their strength, endurance, and quickness during the football season. This led us to the conclusion that the use of both weights and ropes during the season would greatly cut down on these losses.

Since using this program, the loss of strength, endurance, and quickness has nearly been eliminated and the amount of injuries has significantly decreased. The players are much fresher and do not tire as readily in the second half of the season as they had done prior to the program.

INDEX

A

Advantages, 9-11
Aggressiveness, 27
Alignment:
  ends, 81-83
  guards, 45
  halfback, 89-91
  linebackers, 64-66
  safety, 102-106
  tackles, 55-57
Attacks, changes in, 21-27

B

Backfield Defensive Scouting
    Booklet, 176
Blitz:
  linebackers, 74-75
  safety, 104, 109
  secondary, 138
Breakdown position, 63

C

Calls, defensive, 28, 52, 119-121, 144
Changes in opponents' attacks:
  increased running, 21
  wide passing actions, 21-27
Characteristics:
  Combination-60, 27-28
  ends, 40
  guards, 38-39
  halfbacks, 41-42
  linebackers, 40-41
  safety, 42
  tackles, 39
Charts:
  Down and Distance, Field
      Position, 184-187

Chart *(cont'd.)*
  Formation and Play, 180-184
  Individual Pass and Run
      Summary, 187-190
  Offensive Personnel Chart,
      190-192
Cheat Adjustment, 44, 51, 59
Combination Defenses:
  confuse the opponent, 141
  defensive calls, 144
  game specials, 146-147
  goal-line and short-yardage,
      147-154
    Gap, 148-152
    Tough, 152-154
  purpose, 141
  various combinations, 145-146
  what it involves, 28
  when used, 142-144
Combo, 218-220
Corner:
  linebacker, 79
  safety, 102, 107
  secondary, 126-128
Coverages, 29

D

Defensive Calls, 28, 52
Defensive calls:
  Combination Defenses, 144
  Team Defenses, 119-121
Defensive line:
  combo, 219-220
  defensive personnel, 19-20
  drills, 202-206, 214-216, 219-220
  Dummy Wave, 202-203
  group period, 214-218
  Hose Attack, 204-205
  Live Rush, 219-220
  One-on-One, 219

223

Defensive line *(cont'd.)*
    Shiver Slide, 203-204
    Sled Attack, 205-206
    Stop the Run, 215-216
    Technique and Recognition,
        214-215
Direction step, 46
Double-Up:
    ends, 82
    linebackers, 66
Down and Distance, Field Position
    Chart, 184-187
Down the Line, 211-212
Draw and Middle Screen, 72-73
Dummy Wave, 202-203

E

Ends:
    alignment, 81-83
    Double-Up, 82
    drills, 206-212, 216-218
    Gap, 152
    group period, 216-218
    keys and reactions, 83-85
    offside, 82-83, 85, 86-87, 87-88
    onside, 81-82, 83-84, 86, 87
    Pinch, 85
    position description, 40
    run responsibilities, 86-88
    Stack, 82
    stance, 81
    Tough, 153
    Walkaway, 82
Evaluation, post-game, 196-197

F

Features, 28-29
Film Breakdown Form, 179
First kicking period, 213
Formation and Play Chart, 180-184
40-yard dash, 35
Free Safety:
    linebacker, 80
    safety, 103, 108
    secondary, 136-139
Front Defenses:
    Slants, 121-123

Front Defenses *(cont'd.)*
    Up, 123-125

G

Game Plan, 192-194, 194-196
Game specials, 146-147
Gap, 29, 148-152
Goal-line and short-yardage
    defenses, 147-154
Group period, 214-218
Guards:
    alignment, 45
    gap, 152
    keys and reactions, 53-55
    pass responsibilities, 55
    position description, 38-39
    run responsibilities, 55
    stance, 44-45
    technique, 45-52
    Tough, 153-154

H

Halfback:
    alignment, 89-91
    all other zone coverages, 99
    all zone coverages, 95, 96
    Corner, 94, 99
    Corner and Invert, 94
    Gap, 148-150
    Invert, Stay, Free Safety, 94
    keys and reactions, 92-97
    Man-to-Man, 99
    pass responsibilities, 100-101
    position description, 41-42
    run responsibilities, 97-100
    Stalk, 93
    stance, 89
    Stay, Free Safety, 94
    Tough, 152
Halftime, 218
Hose Attack, 204-205

I

Individual Pass and Run Summary,
    187-190

Individual period, 200, 202-213
Information, scouting, 28
Interior line:
  guards, 44-55
    alignment, 45
    keys and reactions, 53-55
    pass responsibilities, 55
    run responsibilities, 55
    stance, 44-45
    techniques, 45-52
  tackles, 55-62
    alignment, 55-57
    keys and reactions, 59-60
    pass responsibilities, 61-62
    run responsibilities, 61
    stance, 55
    techniques, 57-59
Invert:
  linebacker, 79
  safety, 103, 108, 110
  secondary, 128-135
Invert Lou, 121
Invert Red, 121
Isolation block, 72

K

Keys and reactions:
  ends, 83-85
  guards, 53-55
  halfback, 92-97
  linebackers, 66-74
  safety, 106-109
  tackles, 59-60
Kicking period, first, 213

L

Leverage Drill, 207-208
Linebackers:
  alignment, 64-66
  blitz, 74-75
  breakdown position, 63
  Corner, 79
  Double-Up, 66
  Draw and Middle Screen, 72-73
  drills, 206-212, 216-218
  Free Safety, 80
  Gap, 151
  group period, 216-218

Linebackers *(cont'd.)*
  Invert, 79
  Isolation block, 72
  keys and reactions, 66-74
  lack of size, 20-21
  offside, 64, 73-74, 76-77, 78-81
  onside, 64, 67, 75-76, 77-78
  pass responsibility, 77-81
  position description, 40-41
  protect from blockers, 27
  run responsibilities, 75-77
  speed and aggressiveness, 27
  Stack, 65
  stance, 63
  Stay, 79
  tackles, 27
  Tough, 152
  Walkaway, 65
Line Defensive Scouting Booklet,
  176
Live Rush, 219-220
Lock On:
  alignment, 104-105
  keys, 109
  secondary, 138

M

Man-to-Man:
  run responsibilities, 99
  secondary, 139-140
Mental qualities, 31, 32
Mile and one-half run, 37-38

N

Normal:
  alignment, 105
  keys and reactions, 109
  secondary, 138

O

Offensive Personnel Chart, 190-192
Offside:
  ends, 82-83, 85, 86-87, 87-88
  front defender, 28
  linebackers, 64, 73-74, 76-77,
    78-81

Offside *(cont'd.)*
  linemen, 43
Off-tackle play:
  Pinch, 157
  "Slant," 156, 158
  "Slant-Left," 157, 158, 159, 160
  "Slant-Right," 155, 157, 158, 159
  "Up" technique, 159
One-on-One, 219
Onside:
  Defensive Call, 28
  ends, 81-82, 83-84, 86, 87
  linebackers, 64, 67, 75-76, 77-78
  linemen, 43
Opponents' attacks:
  increased running, 21
  wide passing action, 21-27
Option play:
  Free Safety, 163
  Pinch, 163
  reading problems for
      quarterback, 160
  "Slant," 163, 164
  "Slant-Left"—"Corner," 166
  "Slant-Left"—"Free Safety
      Normal," 162
  "Slant-Right"—"Corner," 165
  Stay coverage, 162
  Switch, 163
  Tough—Man-to-Man, 164
  "Up-Left"—"Free Safety Normal,"
      166
  "Up-Left"—"Stay," 163
  "Up-Right," 163
  "Up Right"—"Stay," 161
  "Up" technique, 161
  Walkaway, 163
Option-Tight End Arc, 178

P

Pass responsibilities:
  guards, 55
  halfback, 100-101
  linebackers, 77-81
  safety, 111
  tackles, 61-62
Pass Summary Chart, 188
Personnel:
  daily observation of players, 31
  defensive line, 19-20

Personnel *(cont'd.)*
  freedom of position selection, 32
  linebackers, 20-21
  mental qualities, 31, 32
  physical qualities, 31
  position descriptions, 38-42
    ends, 40
    guards, 38-39
    halfbacks, 41-42
    linebackers, 40-41
    safety, 42
    tackles, 39
  testing program, 31, 32-38
    athletic ability, 32
    first day of fall practice, 32
    40-yard dash, 35
    mile and one-half run, 37-38
    push-ups, 35-36
    side-stepping, 36-37
    team grouped, 32
    vertical jumps, 33-34
    work player has done, 32
Physical qualities, 31
Pinch, 85, 157, 163, 171
Position descriptions:
  ends, 40
  guards, 38-39
  halfbacks, 41-42
  linebackers, 40-41
  safety, 42
  tackles, 39
Post-game evaluation, 196-197
Power Drill, 220
Prevent:
  alignment, 104
  keys and reactions, 109
  secondary, 138
Pursuit and Gang Tackling, 52
Push-ups, 35

R

Read and Step, 208-209
Rope jumping, 222
Running, increased, 21
Run responsibilities:
  ends, 86-88
  guards, 55
  halfback, 97-100
  linebackers, 75-77
  safety, 109-111

Run responsibilities *(cont'd.)*
  tackles, 61
Run Summary Chart, 189

S

Safety:
  alignment, 102-106
  Blitz, 104, 109
  Corner coverage, 102, 107
  Free Safety, 103, 108
  Gap, 150-151
  Invert coverage, 103, 108, 110
  keys and reactions, 106-109
  Lock On, 104-105, 109
  most important, 42
  Normal, 105, 109
  pass responsibilities, 111
  Prevent, 104, 109
  run responsibilities, 109-111
  stance, 101-102
  Stay coverage, 102, 107
  Tough, 152
Scouting:
  adjusting game plan during
    game, 194-196
  *Backfield Defensive Scouting
    Booklet,* 176
  coordinate report and game plan,
    192-194
  Down and Distance, Field Position
    Chart, 184-187
  Film Breakdown Form, 179
  Formation and Play Chart,
    180-184
  Individual Pass and Run
    Summary, 187-190
  Line Defensive Scouting Booklet,
    176
  Offensive Personnel Chart,
    190-192
  "Option—Tight End Arc," 178
  organization of program, 175-180
  Pass Summary Chart, 188
  post-game evaluation, 196-197
  Run Summary Chart, 189
  Scouting Form, 177, 186
  Scout Team Play Cards, 190
  use of information, 28
Scrimmage, 43

Secondary:
  drills, 212-213, 218
  group period, 218
  halfback, 89-101
    alignment, 89-91
    keys and reactions, 92-97
    pass responsibilities, 100-101
    run responsibilities, 97-100
    stance, 89
  safety, 101-111
    alignment, 102-106
    keys and reactions, 106-109
    pass responsibilities, 111
    run responsibilities, 109-111
    stance, 101-102
  Team Defenses, 125-140
    Blitz, 138
    Corner, 126-128
    Free Safety, 136-139
    Invert, 128-135
    Lock-On, 138
    Man-to-Man (regular), 139-140
    Normal, 138
    Prevent, 138
    Stay, 135-136
Shiver Slide, 203-204
Short-yardage defenses, goal-line
  and, 147-154
Shuffle, Peddle, 212-213
Side-stepping, 36
"Slant," 28, 45-60, 121-123, 156,
  158, 163, 164, 168, 169, 171,
  173
Sled Attack, 205-206
Slot Alignment, 58
Speed, 27
Split-End Rule, 56, 58, 59
Sprint pass:
  Pinch technique, 171
  "Slant," 171, 173
  "Slant-Left"—"Invert," 171-172
  "Slant-Tackles Up-Right"—"Free
    Safety Normal," 173
  "Up-Right"—"Corner," 170-171
Stack:
  end, 82
  linebackers, 65
Stalk, 93
Stance:
  ends, 81
  guards, 44-45
  halfback, 89

Stance *(cont'd.)*
  linebackers, 63
  safety, 101-102
  tackles, 55
Stay:
  defensive calls, 120
  linebacker, 79
  safety, 102, 107
  secondary, 135-136
Stop the Run, 215-216
Stretch period, 200

T

Tackles:
  alignment, 55-57
  Gap, 152
  keys and reactions, 59-60
  pass responsibilities, 61-62
  position description, 39
  run responsibilities, 61
  stance, 55
  techniques, 57-59
  Tough, 153
Teaching period, 213-214
Team, 220-221
Team Defenses:
  compare "Slant" to "Up," 116
  confusion for offense, 117
  defensive calls, 119-121
    "Invert Lou," 121
    "Invert Red," 121
    "Stay," 120
  different alignment, 116
  effect on secondary, 114
  front defenses, 121-125
    "Slants," 121-123
    "Ups," 123-125
  problems of blockers, 115
  problems of opponent, 114
  purpose, 114
  questions, 113
  same basic alignment, 115
  same technique in same direction,
    113
  secondary, 125-140
    Blitz, 138
    Corner, 126-128
    Free Safety, 136-139

Team Defenses *(cont'd.)*
    Invert, 128-135
    Lock-On, 138
    Man-to-Man (regular), 139-140
    Normal, 138
    Prevent, 138
    Stay, 135-136
  tendency to run particular play,
    117-118
  what it involves, 28
Technique and Recognition, 214-215
Techniques:
  guards, 45-52
  tackles, 57-59
Testing program:
  administered, 32
  40-yard dash, 35
  mile and one-half run, 37-38
  push-ups, 35-36
  side-stepping, 36-37
  vertical jump, 33-34
  what it indicates, 32
Tough, 29, 152-154
Trap play:
  "Slant," 168, 169
  "Slant-Left Side Up-Right"—
    "Corner," 169, 170
  "Slant-Right"—"Corner," 167
  "Up-Left," 169
  "Up-Left"—"Invert," 168
  "Up" technique, 168
Turn and Catch, 210

U

"Up," 28, 123-125, 159, 161, 168

V

Vertical jump, 33-34

W

Walkaway:
  ends, 82
  linebackers, 65